Choosing the Future

Choosing the Future
The Power of Strategic Thinking

Stuart Wells

Butterworth–Heinemann

Boston Oxford Johannesburg Melbourne New Delhi Singapore

Butterworth–Heinemann

 A member of the Reed Elsevier group

All rights reserved.

∞ Recognizing the importance of preserving what has been written, Butterworth–Heinemann prints its books on acid-free paper whenever possible.

 Butterworth–Heinemann supports the efforts of American Forests and the Global ReLeaf program in its campaign for the betterment of trees, forests, and our environment.

Library of Congress Cataloging-in-Publication Data
Wells, Stuart.
    Choosing the future : the power of strategic thinking / Stuart Wells.
        p.   cm.
    Includes bibliographical references and index.
    ISBN 0–7506–9876–4 (alk. paper)
    1. Strategic planning. I. Title.
    HD30.28.W384 1997
    658.4′012—dc21   97–20071
                                                                CIP

British Library Cataloguing-in-Publication Data
A catalogue record for this book is available from the British Library.

The publisher offers special discounts on bulk orders of this book.
For information, please contact:

Manager of Special Sales
Butterworth–Heinemann
225 Wildwood Avenue
Woburn, MA 01801-2041
Tel: 617-928-2500
Fax: 617-928-2620

For information on all our business publications,
contact our World Wide Web home page at: http://www.bh.com

10 9 8 7 6 5 4 3 2

Printed in the United States of America

CONTENTS

PREFACE

I think, therefore I am.

RENE DESCARTES, *Discourse on Method*

Bookstores are filled with advice on what to think and what to do to succeed. Authors often demonstrate their expertise by giving you answers about what you should do to become excellent, successfully reengineer, effectively use teams, etc. Regardless of the insight and value of their ideas in telling you how to run your business and what you should do, the advice seems to change from year to year. It seems to happen continually, whether encouraged by the authors or not, that their insightful ideas frequently become converted into techniques everyone tries to duplicate, until problems appear and another fad emerges. There is nothing wrong with these fads as they frequently have wonderful thought at their core and show people are struggling to find ways of managing some very challenging issues. There is a problem, however, in giving a one-size-fits-all answer. Learning from the success of other organizations is useful but it is often too late to get competitive advantage from an idea that has become a fad.

In *Management Redeemed*, Frederick Hilmer and Lex Donaldson discuss how these streams of fads continue to undermine rational thought in organizations. Quinn Spitzer and Ron Evans (*Heads You Win*) follow the same line of reasoning, claiming that the latching on to fads or the latest management technique is equivalent to the "outsourcing of thinking." Fads lead managers to believe that off-the-shelf simple solutions are appropriate for problems in complex systems. We need to use the power of our thinking to embrace the complexity we face and find our own solutions and direction for the future.

A problem with fads is that the example is always about someone else's company and their success. By the time you read about it, everyone else (including your competitors) is trying to duplicate the idea. Although it might be a worthy idea in which you want to invest resources, it is no longer sufficient to get an edge for competitive advantage. It is not so much starting the next fad as getting ahead of the curve so someone can study you and use your company as an example. Thinking is the ultimate competitive edge because it causes you to focus on what is possible rather than copying what has been done.

A November 11, 1995 article in *The Economist* stressed the importance of building knowledge in a learning organization and concluded, "Knowledge is market power." The significance of knowledge and intellectual capital to the success of an organization has created substance for the standard phrase, "We value our employees." Ikujiro Nonaka and Hirotaka Takeuchi (*The Knowledge-Creating Company*) focus on "the capability of a company as a whole to create new knowledge, disseminate it throughout the organization, and embody it in products, services and systems." Thomas A. Stewart (*Intellectual Capital*) states that, "Intellectual capital is the sum of everything everybody in a company knows that gives it a competitive edge. . . . Intellectual capital is intellectual material—knowledge, information, property, experience—that can be put to use to create wealth."

Both of these books wonderfully stress the importance of knowledge—what we know. I want to build on that focus on intellectual capital and add thinking—what we do with what we know. Experts know a lot; leaders use thinking to act on what they know. Thinking takes a knowledge base and allows us to look at it through a variety of perspectives. We may always need to know more, but we also need to do more with what we know. We are what we think—the way we think creates what we see and hence the future for which we can conceive a strategy. The only limit to the possibilities of the company is the mind of its people and what they are able to originate.

I would rather follow the old adage of teach someone to fish and you feed them for life. Therefore, I will channel my own efforts to assisting you in learning *how* to think. This is about something more longlasting, something that will enable you to approach any new idea and determine if it fits your organization, something that will allow you to invent your own ideas. This is about your freedom. Freedom can only come through a mind free to think, ask the right questions, and find answers. If you want to lose the possibility of working toward your potential and in a very real sense your humanity, give up your right to think. If you want to reduce someone else's potential or humanity, severely restrict or take away their right to think.

Thinking throws a light of understanding on the past, gives us clarity about the present, and illuminates the possibilities of the future. The *past* has happened. It is real and we cannot change it. Our experiences are important only if we use them to move forward. We can learn from experience; we should not be imprisoned by it. Our effectiveness in the reality of the *present* depends upon our level of awareness and attention, but that is the subject for another book. The *future* is different. It is not real. It only exists in one place—in the mind. It has no substance beyond that. The future is the realm of strategy. The only reason for strategy is to make a deliberate choice about the future. The future is not predetermined; we have choice. We do not have control. Uncertainty is rampant. We know the future will not exactly replicate the past but we frequently act that way because this uncertainty seems insurmountable. In this case, the past becomes a prison rather than a teacher.

I do not have all the answers but I know how to ask a good question. I cannot predict the future but I know how to think. I also know that you know how to think, but 25 years of consulting and college teaching, two Master's degrees, and a Doctorate from Stanford University lead me to realize how little attention we pay to our own thinking. Wanting to succeed, to do things right, to make a contribution, we are easily caught in the ideas of others. There is nothing wrong with your thinking, but odds are you do not give your own thinking enough thought. Albert Einstein said, "The significant problems we face cannot be solved at the same level of thinking we were at when we created them."

The future continually demands a reordering of our thinking so that we do not keep walking down the same well-trodden paths. I am not going to tell you *what* to think. I do not even want to give you one method for *how* to think. I want to encourage the flexibility and freedom of your thought. Maybe we have as much at stake as the rats in the brain experiments described in a February 24, 1996 article in *The Economist*: "The more synapses a nerve cell has, the more ways it has to exchange information with other nerve cells. The more synapses a brain has per nerve cell, the more likely it is that the brain will be able to process and respond to new information. Rats that live in complex environments do indeed develop more synapses between their nerve cells." We need challenge, complexity, and variety in our thinking. We increase our potential when we mentally engage with the complexity of our environment. The more we think, the more we add to the competitive advantage of our business.

In this book I am going to give you an opportunity to develop more synapses by addressing a wide range of different thinking processes for strategy. See them as mental tools that you choose to use as the circumstances warrant.

Strategic thinking can be summed up quite simply:

- What seems to be happening?
- What possibilities do we face?
- What are we going to do about it?

It is not about some cumbersome planning process to emerge with a big document. It is about maintaining an acute sensitivity to changing conditions, an active mind, a willingness to think in a variety of ways, an avoidance of traps formed by what you know, and an ability to decide. Strategic thinking adds increasing depth and perspective to those three questions, but we never want to lose sight of this natural flow of thought.

As you become increasingly adept at moving in and out of different thinking processes, you increase your organization's success in its strategic choices. This is a journey into possibilities, not a guide to one simple answer. Strategic thinking is not a fad but a permanent component of your capability. As conditions change, the old answers crumble. The ability to choose the future through the power of your thinking never fades away.

The booklet for a recent Rene Magritte exhibit at the Montreal Museum of Fine Arts quotes him as saying, "I am not an artist, I am a man who thinks." The exhibit booklet explains that Magritte "saw himself as a thinker who expressed thoughts through painting, regarding his art as a tool for investigating the world." That reflects the ultimate purpose of this book. We are not people in business, but people who think. We choose business as a powerful mechanism to express and realize our thoughts for the future.

In Magritte's paintings, and the creative design on the front of this book, we see that anything is possible. Reality is what we choose; the imagination is not restricted. In business that thought may seem to be an oversimplified exaggeration. There are, however, many more possibilities than we allow our minds to consider. The way we think opens the doorway to the future we can choose. The choices we make today influence the world we will experience tomorrow. We certainly want to choose wisely, but in strategy we want our minds sufficiently free to see the range of possibilities lying in wait just outside our normal vision. Maybe we do want to be what comedian Steven Wright calls a peripheral visionary—"Seeing into the future but way off to the side."

ACKNOWLEDGMENTS

My journey into the world of strategy began nearly 30 years ago at Stanford's Graduate School of Business. I am grateful to two superb people who were my most memorable professors, Hal Eyring and Ed Zschau. More than ten years later I had the good fortune to create lasting friendships and working relationships with two guides of unrelenting thoughtfulness and insight, Jim Clark and Charlie Krone. After a spell of another few years, a different and valuable dimension to my thinking was added when the door to poetry was opened by two emissaries of compassion, Robert Bly and David Whyte. I have been working with the ideas in this book for several years with hundreds of people, creating strategies for their business, starting a new business, or completing a project for their MBA degree. Invariably, I have met many people with high motivation whose engagement with strategic thinking has been beneficial to my development and this work. Through all this time there have been countless ways to thank my wife, Daphne Wells, but now I can choose a simple one—the excellent job she did of editing this manuscript for style and meaning. In bringing this book to fruition I am grateful to Karen Speerstra, Stephanie Gelman Aronson, and Jodie McCune at Butterworth–Heinemann for their ongoing intelligence and enthusiasm.

PART 1

To Think or Not to Think?
That Should Not Be a Question

CHAPTER 1

Closed Mind, Open Mind

Every man takes the limits of his own field of vision for the limits of the world.

ARTHUR SCHOPENHAUER, *Parerga & Paralipomena*

The Fault, Dear Brutus, Lies Not in Our Stars

Just for a moment contemplate the following statement:

Every stumble by a major corporation has occurred in the face of rising product demand.

At first, it does not seem possible. I think, however, you can make a similar statement about any failure regardless of the business's size. I am not saying falling demand or even stagnant demand. When GM, Ford, and Chrysler stumbled, had our passion for vehicles ended? Had the roads suddenly emptied? No. When IBM stumbled, did people suddenly stop buying computers? No. As Apple stumbles, has the market for personal computers dried up? No. We are swimming in computers and new possibilities in the information age. When Pan Am and Eastern disappeared from the skies, had the number of people flying declined? No. When Sears stumbled, had people suddenly stopped shopping? No. As K-Mart stumbles, is the retail discount industry on the ropes? No.

Clearly, there are many examples of this phenomenon—severe business problems in the face of vibrant markets. I know that markets decline and businesses shrink. That is life; it is not a stumble by an organization. Actually, I do not want to join the chorus of corporate-bashing pundits. I am aiming at people, at each of us. How did these stumbles happen? They are not victims of excessive government regulation. They are not victims of unfair foreign competition. They are not victims of unions. These forms of corporate whining are rather tiresome. It is not their fate or their stars. What happened is quite simple and profound— they were out-thought. While they stumbled, others thrived. They are victims of only one thing—their own thought patterns.

Were the people in the organizations stupid? Did they know less than the organizations that did well in these rising demand markets? It is not a lack of information or intelligence but misguided intelligence. It is so simple to become imprisoned by experience and past thoughts. This *little* problem is an everyday occurrence.

Self-Imposed Limits

A friend and I are rebuilding a deck that has a room underneath, so it is really a deck over a flat roof. Rain needs to drain. A previous leak problem caused us to redesign it so that we would have a sealed four-sided box that could safely hold water until it went down the drain pipe. When we had completed three sides, a friend showed up and said it would be a good idea to let that side remain open so the water could flow off into a gutter. We had never thought of that possibility, as our thinking was boxed in both literally and figuratively. On putting in the gutter we decided to put a slight slope on the roof and raise the deck one step above the adjoining deck. By the time we finished, we had an 11-inch step—much too high. My wife suggested a second step within three seconds of having the problem described to her. We had been working on this deck for only a few days. We had no real stake in our design. We had no strong investments. We had not built our career around it. Yet, our thinking was locked into patterns formed by our initial ideas.

An NBC news story on February 19, 1996 reported a new form of bypass surgery that is minimally invasive. It requires only a small three-inch cut in the skin. It is not necessary to stop the heart and connect the patient to a machine to artificially replicate the heart and lung functions. Recovery takes only three days in the hospital rather than eight days for normal bypass operations. This procedure is useful for many but not all heart problems requiring bypass surgery. When the reporter asked the surgeon why they were not doing this procedure five years ago, he responded, "We didn't think of it." Not, "We still needed to develop the technology, equipment, etc." Not, "We lacked the knowledge or capability." They didn't think of it.

To Mark Twain, familiarity breeds contempt. I would say familiarity breeds closed minds. Intelligent, highly trained, experienced people lose their insight into new possibilities because of their high level of involvement. If I could miss useful ideas after only a few days of work on a project, imagine the problem in business, where people have years of experience, detailed knowledge, and high levels of motivation. Every fiber of our being becomes locked into the past. Every example I mentioned can be traced to this simple problem—the powerful thoughts that brought you success in the past do not serve you in the future as conditions change. I am not talking about skills, experience, or knowledge. I am talking about the thinking processes we apply to these.

In a February 22, 1996 interview on the National Public Radio program *Fresh Air*, Steve Jobs was asked about the failure of Next in creating a new generation of computers. He attributed the failure to trying to operate from the same "paradigms of success" that had worked so well with Apple. The company did create a technologically superior computer, but the world had moved on and this was not what the market craved in large numbers. Experience had misguided his thinking, keeping it tied to the past rather than moving toward the future. The world had changed, but his thinking had not.

Microsoft seemed headed to the same disaster as they "were thinking like rational engineers, assuming that computer users would prefer the faster response, better sound, and crisper graphics of CD-ROM over the barely controlled chaos of the Internet" (*Fast Company*, June:July 1996). Now there is a massive commitment of resources within Microsoft to Internet-oriented products. "Bill Gates has been intensely aware of how other market-leading companies have stumbled when their top executives failed to read the signs of fundamental change in their industries" (*Business Week*, July 15, 1996). This article is a wonderful account of how persistent people, other than Gates, had to combat prevailing patterns of thought, eventually causing Gates to see the future through new eyes and redirect the company. Win or lose on the Internet, it is a wonderful example of how a company can change if its people can alter their thinking. In the radio interview, Steve Jobs said Apple had a ten-year lead on Microsoft but didn't sustain it and let them catch up. He felt they need to be 100 percent better in a Microsoft-Intel world and are only 5 percent better. I would say they need to accelerate their thinking.

The Horror of the Situation

Nevertheless, the problem of inflexible thinking is still quite widespread. Why is it so hard to eliminate the damage caused by our own thinking?

- We do not teach thinking.
- We want instant solutions and quick closure.
- We do not tolerate thinking.
- We have no patience for thinking.
- We pride ourselves on our practicality.
- We remain enslaved by our own thoughts.

There is no chance for sustaining competitive advantage in the turbulent, complex conditions we face without unleashing the power of people's thinking. Why did communism fail? It is not a problem of government control versus private control, regardless of the propaganda you want to believe. People run institutions. Stifle the thinking of people in archaic, bureaucratic structures and you will collapse. Try to motivate by compulsion and fear and you will collapse. Stay locked in yesterday's successful thinking and you will collapse. There is no freedom without freed thinking. Eliminate all the institutional constraints on the free flow of thought and we are still left with our personal boundaries to an open and free mind. Until we focus, individually, on the way we think, we remain enslaved to ourselves.

Take a Test, Win a Diploma

From the day we enter school, thinking takes a back seat to skills and memory. My wife has been teaching kindergarten or first grade since 1970. She constantly has parents proudly telling her how well their children read. Their standard for reading is word recognition. Her standard goes much further. Recognition is a necessary skill; children must remember the letters and the different combinations they make to form words, but reading is ultimately about comprehension. How does the child mentally engage with the written word? Skills and memory are a precursor to the development of thinking. If children develop a love for reading along with the mechanics and see reading as a valuable effort rather than a required effort, they will have their thinking engaged. Thinking shifts reading from a passive to an active endeavor. As adults, we know it is different to read a magazine, a novel, a poem, or a work in philosophy. Each requires a different engagement with our brain, although I suspect many of us treat the process in the same way regardless of the content.

We are so busy ensuring that students accumulate increasing bits of information and testing their ability to replicate it, that we leave little room for thinking in the curriculum. The problem is not confined to the frequently maligned public schools. It exists from kindergarten through the highest levels of universities. Teaching and testing focus most heavily on facts and content knowledge. The creative and deliberate deployment of alternative ways to think about the facts and content is difficult to measure or test. So they remain in the background. Even in a highly interactive classroom environment, it is the rapid thinker whose hand is recognized. People think in different ways and at different speeds. Without explicit treatment of alternative thinking processes, we build barriers to approaches that do not seem to fit in with the established order. The result is an unplanned exclusion of the insights of some students or, more pointedly, some participants in business meetings.

Do not despair. All is not bleak. We do learn to think. It is just that thinking is not an explicit topic. If you study any subject you will learn a method of thinking, a view of the world, regardless of the method used to present the content. For example, I have an undergraduate degree in mechanical engineering. When I decided to move my career in a different direction, friends and, needless to say, relatives, thought I had wasted my time in my studies. They were seriously mistaken. Whether I used engineering knowledge again or not, I had learned something far more valuable that even the professors did not consciously address—a logical, analytical process for solving complex problems. This is an extremely useful mental discipline; it is not the only way of thinking.

Think of different functional responsibilities of people in the organization. You can ask people what they do in marketing, but it is also clear that they have a different way of thinking about things than people in production, finance, or personnel. Each discipline brings its own valid way of viewing the world, thinking about problems, and understanding information. Often real business situations require a blending of these thinking processes, and meetings become frustrating because we have never learned to articulate the way we think. This lack of articulation leads us to assume unconsciously that we have the correct way of seeing things and that the other dullards are incapable of understanding. With an explicit appreciation for different thinking styles, many of these interpersonal problems would evaporate.

Answers 5¢, Questions $1

Several years ago I visited Mt. Madonna Center in Watsonville, California, a retreat facility with a resident community and resident guru, Baba Hari Dass, who has chosen silence. At 5:00 A.M. on Saturdays the community and interested visitors gather in an informal session with him. People ask him questions and he writes a brief response on a small hand-held blackboard. This environment inspired me to think of provocative questions. As I contemplated whether I would trouble him with my question and waited for other people to ask their questions, I noticed I would start to answer my own question only to come to another, more challenging question. Before I had the courage to ask him this second question, my mind would again enter an answering process, ultimately coming to another question. This process passed through several iterations, allowing me to discover things I might not have understood had I wanted him to spoon-feed me answers. I left, valuing the experience but also wondering why people would ask him questions just to get answers and why they did not take the time to seek their own responses.

There is one other negative impact of schooling that permeates our behavior everywhere—we want answers. We do not want questions. We want quick problem solving and immediate results. The last thing we want is a thought-provoking question, even though the side of us that loves learning wants this type of challenge. School requires answers—not any old answers, the correct answers. No one has ever gotten high grades for asking questions. Students fear questions because they may not have the right answer. They want to know what the right answer is. They do not trust the answers of their fellow students until the teacher acknowledges what is correct. The normal classroom does not seem very different from the Mt. Madonna retreat center, except that the teacher has a bigger blackboard and does most of the talking.

There is no value for the exploration that a good question could create. There is no value for being in an answering process guided by challenging questions that will help us reveal unexpected answers. We believe that our ability to respond correctly reveals the level of our intelligence. Tests demand answers. It certainly does take intelligence to sift through data and come to a conclusion. We need to have an equally high regard for the intelligence to ask challenging questions. We need to drop our illusion of expertise as solely demonstrated by rapid dexterity in giving answers. Innovations that move us forward derive from the questioning mind.

In business, time is of the essence. Often we surround ourselves with complex, painful, time-consuming rituals because we believe in hard work. We are filling time on the clock and everything is important. No time is idle or wasted. Often in the ritual following our belief system nothing of lasting consequence happens. The present is managed to the detriment of the future. We have full plates, packed schedules, and no time for diversions. We need answers and we need them now. A question will divert our attention from the task at hand. You should have an idea (an answer) and the ability to defend it against the kind of questions that may undermine your idea. This form of debate process, putting ideas and proposals under close scrutiny, is useful but it is not the kind of questioning that opens new possibilities. Thinking in business requires a powerful ability to ask tough questions—the kind that are difficult to answer. An easily answered question is not worth anything. An answer creates no challenge for the brain. A good question means you must take time. A good question must provoke thought; when we finally come to an answer, we feel as if we have challenged ourselves. Without questions there is no strategy. There are no answers about the future. We want challenging questions to open strategic possibilities so that our decision reflects the widest possible vision. A strategy is not the correct answer; it is our best thinking given the quality of the questions we ask.

You're Not Paid to Think

Sit down at your desk. Don't do anything. Don't move any papers. Think about something important to your job. How long do you think you can sit there before someone wonders what you are doing? Why are you wasting time, not doing anything? If you are really lucky, your boss will walk by and when you respond to the inquiry that you are thinking you will receive the time-honored response—you're not paid to think. Then again, maybe you're the person walking by and that is your response. Do we have a more destructive phrase in business? If they really meant it, it is only a matter of technological advance to move you to the unemployment line. What they usually mean is—we lack the capability to provoke and channel thinking and do not know how to create the environment that allows appropriate time for thinking.

Let's face it. We do not want people thinking. We want them acting, doing things. The open cubicle design of many offices is a sure sign that thinking is not necessary. You need to learn tricks to think. Move papers around your desk. Let your hand write frantically on a pad, even scribbles. You must keep your body in convincing motion to find the time to think. Or, as the character George Costanza said on the television show "Seinfeld," keep looking at papers on your desk with a concerned but slightly annoyed expression in order to create the impression of being busy. The irony of this somewhat bizarre situation is that thinking is a fast process. It is cheap. In a small amount of time your mind is able to cover an amazing amount of terrain. The only expense is your time, no investments, no other costs.

I am not talking about hours and hours of thinking every day at work. It is hard to sustain thinking for a long time. For the mind, 15 minutes of focused thought can be a long time. Ask someone who has ever tried meditation. Do me a favor. Try to sit for one minute and think. How many different thoughts can your mind cover? When I tried this with a group of people, sitting silently when they expected me to speak, within 20 seconds someone had lost his patience and questioned what was happening. Maybe even a minute of thinking is too much.

In the *Fresh Air* interview, Steve Jobs was also asked about the culture of Apple. He felt it was a fairly typical organization—they had a hierarchy of authority, they were driven to earn money to reinvest in the future. There was one key difference—they did not believe there was a hierarchy of ideas. He said, "We did not pay people to tell them what to do. We paid them to tell us what to do." Even with this apparent value for thinking, it would still be difficult to sustain it in an organization setting. No one can determine when a person will most productively think. You cannot mandate a special time for thinking. We value people's thinking by giving them some degree of flexibility in their daily schedule. If you are not paying people to think, you have no hope for the future.

Stop Beating a Dead Horse to Reinvent the Wheel

One way we find time to think is by scheduling meetings. Meetings have a variety of purposes, but during them action ceases. In sharing information, discussing possible courses of action, and making decisions, there is ample opportunity for thinking. You can always count on someone saying *stop beating a dead horse* or *let's not reinvent the wheel* when they become impatient with the process of the meeting. There are certainly times when these statements are appropriate and discussion needs to cease. These comments also happen when people are unwilling to listen to the ideas of others, contributing greatly to the difficulty in having meetings that value exploratory thinking. One of the great purposes of meetings should be the interaction of people's thinking. We can think independently but the power of focusing two or more intelligent people on a topic is overwhelming. They inspire each other's thoughts, accomplishing significantly more than individuals thinking on their own.

As a small afterthought, I find the notion of *reinventing the wheel* quite fascinating. A few months ago I was playing in a golf foursome and in talking about life and work found out that one of the people was an executive with the company that had been first to put luggage on wheels. That was interesting, as I thought cavemen had invented the wheel for precisely that purpose. For 15,000 years we have been dragging our luggage around because nobody wanted to *reinvent the wheel*. We became more focused on carrying capacity and protection of the goods inside. Were it up to us we probably would have carried the rock for Stonehenge and the pyramids on our backs. Now we are putting wheels on everything—golf travel bags and large ice chests. Why did our thinking fail us for so long on such an obvious use of humankind's first major invention? Probably because every time people had a meeting in a luggage company someone halted thinking by saying, *let's not reinvent the wheel*—and they never did.

I'll skip the story on beating a dead horse, as that is a little too gruesome.

We're Practical People Here

The final block to using thinking effectively is the incredibly misguided belief that there is a dichotomy between theory and practice. *Those who can, do. Those who can't, teach.* More than anything, this statement symbolizes the separation we have created between theory and practice. It shows how little we value the world of the intellect and how often the world of the intellect looks upon practitioners with disdain. It is useless to remain in the world of theory without any practical applications. In business we are in the real world; we need to be practical—no time for the theoretical, the conceptual, the abstract. It is impossible, however, to be truly practical without entering the world of theory and ideas. It is simply wrong to confine the theoretical to the halls of universities. The most impractical thing you could ever do is act as if your view of reality is the only correct one for now and forever into the distant future. The practical is the present, what is currently happening. Theory, the means of conceptually explaining reality, is helpful for understanding the possibilities of the future.

Is it practical to assume implicitly that the future will be the same as the present? Is it practical to limit one's possibilities for the future? Is it practical to design a strategy from one frame of reference? Practical should mean giving one's self and the business the best possible chance to succeed. Those who forget the past are doomed to repeat it. Those who forget to think about the future are doomed to neglect it. Keep your mantra about the real world, practicality, and always being hands-on and you are on the path of stumbling. Thought precedes action. Theory precedes the practical.

On the other hand, we must always place a practical standard on theory, ideas, abstractions, and thinking. We must gain increased insight into the world, industry, and markets surrounding the business. We must gain increasing foresight about possibilities for the future. We must be in a better position to choose a future path that seems to give the business the best hope for a significant competitive advantage. We can outact and outcompete only by outthinking our competitors. Let's change the expression to *Those who can, think and do. Those who can't, think or do but never both.*

Enslaved by Past Thought

The great jazz saxophonist Rahsaan Roland Kirk chanted, "Oh volunteered slavery, it's something we all know." We may know it, but we underestimate how powerful our previous thought is in governing our future thought.

> The great sage was near death and people from all the villages gathered near the death bed. They kept encouraging the person closest to the sage to ask the question before death ended their chance of knowing. Finally, this person said, "Excuse me to disturb you at this moment but we want to know. What is the meaning of life?" The sage looked up, thinking deeply, and responded, "Life is like a river." People nearby wanted to know what the sage had said. The words were passed from one person to the next like the waves rippling outward from a pebble dropped in a pond. "Life is like a river." "What wisdom." "What insight." "What a great sage." Finally, on the far reaches of the crowd an adult turned to a small child and shared the wisdom, "Life is like a river." The child thought for a moment, looked up, and said, "I don't get it. What does it mean, 'Life is like a river'?" The adult couldn't respond. The murmuring of the crowd reversed itself, like waves flowing back to where the pebble had dropped, with people saying, "What does the sage mean?" "I don't know." Finally, it reached the person closest to the sage, who reluctantly but expectantly said, "Excuse me again for disturbing you at this time but what does it mean, 'Life is like a river'?" The sage looked up with deep eyes at the person and said, "Okay, so life isn't like a river."

There are many questions to ask you about this story related to this discourse on thinking. Here is a simple one, but please do not look back to the story. What is the gender of the child, the adult near the child, the person near the sage, and the sage?

Can you see how much your prior thought patterns cause you to make assumptions? There are no gender pronouns in the story. Your mind supplied the gender of the participants. It would not be surprising if your assumptions about gender violated your own belief system about men and women.

This is an everyday experience. We have prior patterns of thought, so deeply ingrained that we pay no attention to them, that can profoundly affect the way we think. Our minds are always operating, filled with deliberately chosen thinking or patterns of which we remain vaguely aware. If we do not value thinking, giving people time for it, encouraging it, talking about how people are thinking as much as what they are thinking, we remain enslaved. Although William

Stafford had a slightly different idea in mind in his poem, *A Ritual to Read to Each Other*, his ending stanza captures the importance of breaking the bonds of our own prior thought.

> For it is important that awake people be awake,
> or a breaking line may discourage them back to sleep;
> the signals we give—yes or no, or maybe—
> should be clear: the darkness around us is deep.

CHAPTER 2

Hey Buddy, Can You Paradigm?

It is strange to see with how much passion
People see things only in their own fashion!

MOLIERE, *The School for Wives*

Convictions are more dangerous enemies of truth than lies.

FRIEDRICH NIETZSCHE, *Human, All Too Human*

Here we are, early in the book, and we have already plunged into overused jargon. If you haven't heard or used the word *paradigm* in the last week or month, you probably haven't been at work. Even the dictionary does not help us—*a paradigm is a model, pattern, standard, or example.* We receive no new insights from the word's origin this time. It would be great if the definition read *a paradigm is a set of beliefs or assumptions about the way the world works that directs the way we think about things. Our prior experiences form paradigms, reflecting our preconceived notions. Sometimes they become so deeply ingrained within us that we forget a paradigm is only one view of reality or the truth. At its best, it gives us a way of making sense and finding order in a complex world; it helps inform our thinking. At its worst, it inhibits us from seeing things from a different perspective; it blocks our thinking.* No such luck, that is not the official definition. For lack of a better word, however, I'll follow the crowd and use it with the meaning we all seem to instill within it.

It may be jargon but it is the most useful word we use to jar thinking. Don't let its overuse constrain you from its essential message. Everything you see and think is potentially a product of your past. Paradigms are the prior patterns of thought I referred to in the last chapter that keep us in volunteered slavery. An underlying theme of this book is increasing the ability to think—breaking the bonds of our own paradigms when they do not fully serve our interest. We seek the ability to move among different paradigms in order to gain various perspectives and develop insight into the environment of the business and strategic possibilities that we could miss if we remained locked in one paradigm.

Reengineering is a valuable approach if it enables you to see your business constructed by a few key processes. It gives you a different way of comprehending how your business is functioning and how it could change to better position itself for the future. Core competency is a wonderful paradigm that has you see your business through the eyes of key skill sets that people collectively maintain in the organization and can bring to bear on a variety of products. Each of these two paradigms has you see your business in a different light from the way you would see it had you retained only a focus on products and their future development. There is nothing wrong with the old paradigms. They served us well and still give us a coherent view of the world. It is simply not the only view. A product focus is important, but to be successful in strategy we need our thinking to allow us to contemplate alternative views. We need to imbue our mind with contrasting paradigms and see what they reveal about the world, what possibilities they open to our view, what alternatives they give us for strategic pursuits. It is a major strategic lever to have the ability to articulate the paradigms that drive behavior in one's industry and comprehend what these views inhibit others from thinking or doing. We explore this issue in detail in Chapter 19. Staying locked in one paradigm, one view of reality is as damaging to your business as taking one cultural perspective as the only valid depiction of truth and thinking that any other culture is misguided.

My concern in this brief chapter is to recognize the power that paradigms hold over us, even as you read this book. There is not a single word I can choose in this book—strategy, competition, goal—that does not immediately evoke some image or thought on your part. A word represents a whole system thought. The dictionary definition merely provides the seed of a starting point. We can probably agree to accept the definition and have a common base to start from, but the way that seed blossoms depends upon our different experiences. *Strategy* may have one definition upon which we agree, although I have seen groups spend considerable time trying to mutually grasp the word's meaning. The paradigms we have about strategy, our systems of thought, can diverge greatly from one another. We bring related knowledge to the word, thoughts about what we should value about the word, thoughts about how well the word has worked in our organizations, and our successes and failures. I am not inventing language or using some new, clever, catchy phrases in this book. I only hope that as you see what appears to be familiar—*been there, done that*—you will contemplate things long enough to see if they offer you some insights different from your own paradigms. I do not want to have you attach yourself to a new paradigm other than this—*the organization's success is completely dependent upon our ability to devote ongoing attention to wide-ranging and flexible thinking.*

CHAPTER 3

Looking for Answers in All the Wrong Places

A sudden, bold, and unexpected question doth many times surprise a man and lay him open.

FRANCIS BACON, *Essays*

An answer is always a form of death.

JOHN FOWLES, *The Magus*

It is not the answer that enlightens, but the question.

EUGENE IONESCO, *Découvertes*

Some Initial Thoughts

For more years than I care to remember and for more times than I care to count, I have sat in audiences listening to someone speak or been in the front of the room speaking. I have heard some wonderfully intriguing ideas. I hope I have provoked thought in others. Inevitably, however, a speaker will say to the audience, "Are there any questions?" It is remarkable how much silence this question evokes in others. Sitting in an audience, I wonder why I do not have a question to grasp this opportunity to engage with this speaker. Standing before an audience I wonder what I have done to inspire this silent response.

It is the fear of looking ignorant that inhibits most of us. After all, a question means—I don't know. If you did know, you would have the answer and not need a question. When the speaker asks a question of the audience, few will respond. That is why we have so many teachers who answer their own questions. Students sit there with poker faces, afraid of any movement, as if they were at an auction and the slightest nod would mean a bid. They fear that if they answer one question, they will get a follow-up question that will eventually reveal their ignorance.

In contrast, when my mother-in-law was a student at Cornell University, a graduate student came to deliver a guest lecture. The presentation went so well that the students did have many questions. To the first question the lecturer responded, "I don't know." To the second question the lecturer responded, "I don't know." Finally, after this pattern was embarrassing everyone, the lecturer said, "I already told you everything I know."

Firmly embedded in my mind is a workshop series I attended over a period of many years led by a close friend and colleague. One of the particularly bright participants always had remarkably challenging questions. The questions were so deep that one wondered why he had so many, why they came in such rapid succession, and why one or two of the questions weren't sufficient for further contemplation. In a rather exasperated but deliberate state, my friend belatedly said, "I won't answer any more of your questions; you haven't done anything with the answers I already gave you."

I have told you the story about the Mt. Madonna community with the guru who has chosen silence. People certainly had no admonitions about asking questions. The respect for the answers of the guru was palpable. This hope for an answer, particularly when the speaker is held in relative awe, stops thinking. I still wonder whether they had the will to engage with their own questions. How much better would it have been if he had written questions on his little backboard rather than answers? Fortunately, he did have a talent for writing the kind of answer that would challenge anyone to think further, if they were so inclined. Unless the answers were swallowed whole, they had gaps, they didn't resolve or kill the issue, there were possibilities to pursue the question further. A good answer does lead to an even deeper question.

> "Are there any questions?" An offer that comes at the end of college lectures and long meetings. Said when an audience is not only overdosed with information, but when there is no time left anyhow. At times like that you sure do have questions. Like "Can we leave now?" and "What the hell was this meeting for?" and "Where can I get a drink?"
>
> The gesture is supposed to indicate openness on the part of the speaker, I suppose, but if in fact you do ask a question, both the speaker and the audience will give you drop-dead looks. And some fool—some earnest idiot—always asks. And the speaker always answers. By repeating most of what he has already said. But if there is a little time left and there is a little silence in response to the invitation, I usually ask the most important question of all: "What is the meaning of life?"
>
> ROBERT FULGHUM, *It Was on Fire When I Lay It Down*

What Is a "Question"?

Life is like a river; that was the sage's answer to the brief story in Chapter 1. When the people were unable to understand this answer because they were unwilling to think, they had another question, asking the sage to deliver the meaning to them. No question is truly important if all one seeks is a quick response.

Answers are death; questions are life. We can never get to the future through answers. We can never get to the future if the only questions we ever ask are ones for which we are mostly seeking information. *What time is it?* That is not a true question. We must divide questions into two simple categories—informational and thought provoking. The informational question category includes anything for which an answer is immediately or easily attainable from some existing information source. The lecturer who answers the questions of the audience is doing a service in imparting information but a disservice in challenging thinking. When my mother-in-law's lecturer had *told them everything he knew*, the possibility existed for something more significant. Now the students and lecturer had something important to learn as they engaged with the answering process.

As rapidly as possible when we are dealing with any thinking process, strategic or otherwise, we need to disclose our knowledge so we get to the frontier of what we know, the place where questions should drive us. It is an oversimplification to say that Martin Heidegger in his book *What Is Called Thinking?* equates thinking with questions, but it certainly is one of his major intentions. Throughout this book, which is a series of lectures, he never really answers the question of his title. What would we do with the answer? We do not know thinking from the answer; we know it by doing it.

Similarly, in any attempt to grapple with a choice about the future, a challenge that carries its own ambiguities, complexities, and unknowns, we must develop the ability to remain in an answering process. It is not so much equating questions with thinking but the struggle to respond that is the place of our thinking. We need the discipline to face our own ignorance, to stand on the threshold of our own knowledge pondering, wondering, seeking. We need to ask the kind of questions to which the first response is that small voice inside us that, partially in fear, responds, *I don't know.* Ignorance is not bliss. Challenging our ignorance so we can move the boundary of our knowledge forward is bliss.

If we ask questions for which we or someone else already has the answer, then we are taking already conceived thoughts and fitting them to the questions. Questions must generate new thought. Thinking is the pursuit of the right questions so that we will engage in answering processes to guide us to new insights and innovative action. It is not about finding one answer or many answers but about having sufficient thought to see the realm of possibilities and then choosing a path that we can never know with certainty is the *right answer.* I have watched people stumble at the first sign of not understanding something and retreat into a patient or irritated state waiting for an answer to arrive—*waiting for roast pigeon to fly into their mouths.*

THOUGHT, I love thought.
But not the juggling and twisting of already existing ideas
I despise that self-important game.
Thought is the welling up of unknown life into consciousness,
Thought is the testing of statements on the touchstone of the conscience,
Thought is gazing onto the face of life, and reading what can be read,
Thought is pondering over experience, and coming to a conclusion.
Thought is not a trick, or an exercise, or a set of dodges,
Thought is a man in his wholeness wholly attending.

D. H. LAWRENCE, *Thought*

Strategy is like the search for the Holy Grail; it is like the continual asking of the question, *what is the meaning of life?* If we are unable to live in the ambiguity and uncertainty of the question, if we must have an answer, then we cannot continue the quest. For strategy is simultaneously a quest without end and the discipline to act in the midst of thought, in the face of questions. We cannot wait for the *right answer* and we cannot naively accept the first answer that comes along. The idea of strategy is being immersed in thought, asking provocative questions, engaging in trying to find answers, and acting decisively even though the answer is not fully formed. You must accept the best answer you have at the moment, assuming your thinking is engaged. You are not settling for an answer but acting while continuing to think. The world will not wait for thinking to end. To end thinking simply because you must act negates the whole power of strategic thinking. It is an ongoing, natural flow of thought evoked by questions.

- What seems to be happening?
- What possibilities do we face?
- What are we going to do about it?

These are real questions as they clearly do not have a simple, easy-to-find answer; they do, however, lead to the demand to act. Business goes on but the quest must continue. We all know strategy is not hammered into tablets and delivered to the group but we frequently act that way, clinging to the answer and being less tolerant of further questions. It is better to see ourselves sufficiently decisive to act in the face of our best thinking than to tire of thinking, stop asking questions, and lock ourselves into the last answer. Thinking implies dissatisfaction with the last answer; it is always searching for deeper insight, something new, some way to do better than we have in the past.

Knowing How to Ask

Ask a Major Question

You must choose something that truly matters. A question for which you do not have a simple answer. A question for which you will not leap to a single answer and that will allow you to think seriously about your response.

What will the future be?
(How is the world our organization faces changing?)

What are people seeking, hoping for, expecting, fearing?
(Why do people buy our products and services?)

How will people cope with and benefit from changes in the future?
(How might customers' needs for our products change?)

What are the possible ways of contributing to the future?
(What must we absolutely, positively do to succeed?)

What is the meaning of life?
(Why are we in this business?)

As you contrast the first question in each series with the second question in parentheses, you can see that the questions have very different impacts on our thinking. We would often think that the first question evokes philosophical discussions best conducted in the evening over a beer, or by some think tank, but out of place with the demands of everyday work. The second question seems more focused and pertinent to a strategy question.

I say both are important; both are real questions for which answers are not readily apparent. It is, however, much easier to roll out answers we already have for the second question than to allow those questions to move us to think into new terrain. The first question, with its relative lack of structure and boundaries, creates a different context for thinking about the second question than occurs if we leap directly into it. It is certainly true that the first question is not one we would use on a frequent, everyday basis, but we must address it from time to time.

Make Sure You Understand the Question

You know when you form a vision or mission statement that you carefully consider each word. As discussed in Chapter 2, words have meaning, serious meaning, in that they evoke images in our mind. These images lead us to a certain train of thought. I do not want to encourage a degeneration into wordsmithing but we must be aware of how we set the context for our own thinking through the words we choose in a question. Each word in the question itself sets up a field of thought and therefore a certain path to an answer. You need to find what you are really asking. As the old saying goes, *be careful of what you ask for, you may get it*. In this case it would be, *be careful of what you ask, it is the only thing you can think about*.

There is a question above that contains the word *customer* in it. Maybe that word immediately evokes in your mind the thought of anyone who buys your product. Do you want to consider potential buyers of your product? Is there a difference between the user and purchaser of the product? Are there others who benefit from the product without being a purchaser or a direct user?

We need to be sure that we have the real question. We all have experiences in problem solving in which we get on the wrong track because we have not defined the right problem. For example, suppose you have high employee turnover. If it is a perceived problem you try to fix it through things like better hiring screening, counseling, training, or job opportunities—you try to find something to improve. It is quite logical to take this cause-effect approach to problem solving. It is the original question, however, that drove you to this line of thought. What if you asked, *why do we want turnover reduced? How can we turn the current rate or increased rates of turnover to our advantage?* You would be on a different line of thought. A question directs your thinking in a manner similar to a paradigm— it opens a particular system of thought.

Ask the Question in Different Ways

Some questions just make you want to think and some kill your energy. Sometimes you just want to answer it and move on.

> *Where did you go? Out. What did you do? Nothing.*

On the other hand, maybe the question is too broad or doesn't give you enough of a hook to draw you in. Even if the question is important, it may not provide sufficient focus for thinking.

> *How can we improve our operations?*

If we find ourselves dully searching for an answer, we may need a different question to enliven our thinking spirit.

> *What do we need to eliminate?*
> *What is most important to our customers?*
> *What are we doing when we are at our best?*

These questions direct our thinking toward alternative interpretations of the word *improve*.

Find Connected Questions

A connected series of questions is often the best approach to a major or more general question. I am definitely an advocate of thinking in frameworks or structures; the mental tools throughout this book are examples of this approach. A framework is a series of questions leading to complete thought about a topic. There is certainly a natural process of the beginning of an answer to one question leading to another question, as happened with my experience in Watsonville. I am suggesting something different here—a design for thinking that you deliberately choose ahead of time. You may find yourself adding, eliminating, or modifying questions as you proceed, but you are attempting to have your design anticipate the kinds of things you want to think about. You are also choosing boundaries for thinking—a question both provokes thought and creates boundaries for it. Good thinking is not about wandering all over the place paying attention to anything that pops into your mind; that can border on being a useless process. I must tell you that it takes discipline to pay attention to the design of a series of connected questions without jumping to answer, or worse, allowing some desired answers to determine the questions you will ask.

Ask Questions in the Context of What Is Already Known

It is totally useless to have a question that merely has you conjuring up already present thoughts. Get your knowledge base explicit. You want to build on that knowledge base to explore new terrain. You want questions to push the boundaries of your knowledge—to cause you to go out and learn more, to cause you to pursue expansion of your knowledge base. Do not ask questions for which you already know the answers. Use what you know to challenge what you think you know—put pressure on your own assumptions, beliefs, and paradigms. Use what you know to expand your horizons—place value on your experience and knowledge rather than finding fault with the present state. Thinking is an issue not of finding fault with what is but of pursuing what could be.

Choose an Answering Process

The last step in this series of ideas for creating questions is to think about the answering process ahead of time. The most important issue from a thinking perspective is how to remain in the quest without succumbing to the pressure of quick answers. Whenever I am in a meeting in which the agenda calls for a decision on an issue, I realize that we are not going to entertain any new questions or additional thinking. The agenda demand may call for some cleverness in organizing thoughts we already have to arrive at a decision, but there is no leeway for new challenges. I know this will sound a little strange but a successful answering process, when you want to think, is to determine the best way to restrain coming to an answer. Have faith. Good questions that provoke thought, combined with the discipline to remain in the process of answering, will always lead to some answer that you can act upon.

CHAPTER 4

What's the Sound
of One Mind Thinking?

*No man is an island, entire of itself; every man is a piece of the
continent.*

JOHN DONNE, *Devotions*

Me and My Shadow

It is the sound of silence; there is very little physical activity. The deeper the
thought, the more the body becomes still. The parent in us wants to say, *it's too
quiet; there must be a problem.* It's not that thinking is some heavy, serious state
but it is not boisterous either. In sleep, the *right* brain, neglected during the day
for the demands of schedules and tasks, explodes in the vibrant images of dreams.
With any luck, the right brain has insights into problems we have been struggling
with all day. Meditation is a fully awake state that reveals much about the sound
of one mind. Many people think of meditation as sitting cross-legged on a floor
trying to achieve nothingness. I see it as practice to turn the mind from the noise
of nearly random thought to the relative calm of focused thought. Meditation
often proceeds from a seed thought or subject, allowing one's mind to build ideas
around that seed, following it to whatever paths open up. It is not the mind
wandering aimlessly but allowing exploration bounded only by the original seed.
There is little attempt at controlling one's mind, other than inattention to the
distraction of peripheral thoughts that seem to keep showing up. It is the ability
to sustain focus that allows one to grasp the full flowering of complexity that
the seed generates.

There is certainly value to the meditative approach for one mind, but I have been moving toward something different—the use of some structure or framework that takes us through a series of questions or connected topics to enrich thinking. The reason is simple; although thinking has a strong individual tone to it, strategic thinking regularly requires people to be working together. Given the extent of the knowledge base in one's business and the complexity of the world surrounding the business, it is unlikely that any single individual has enough understanding to work purely independently. The skill of thinking together is crucial for the strategic success of any organization. Furthermore, although contemplative thinking has its place, strategic thinking invariably must lead us to a decision we have the commitment to follow. As we celebrate the power of the individual human mind, we must also remember how hard it is to keep ourselves honest. Sometimes the sound of one mind thinking is the self-fulfilling prophesy we experience when we bow before the altar of our own prejudices, paradigms, and preconceived notions. We need someone else to jostle us awake. We need others to keep us on track, and so we invented meetings.

> To every meeting there is a season, and a time for every purpose,
> a time to plant and a time to reap
> a time to tear down and a time to build up
> a time to keep silent and a time to speak
> a time to follow an agenda and a time to think
> a time to vote and a time to talk.

Let's Get on Each Other's Calendars

The last time I looked it was difficult to talk and think at the same time; it's even difficult to walk and chew gum at the same time. It's frequently a challenge to listen and think at the same time. If we hear something intriguing, we want to think about it. The difficulty in managing our own thinking while we are trying to speak or listen and the pressing business needs of the moment have frequently pushed thinking to the corner in meetings. We criticize people if their meetings do not come to clear conclusions and seem to wander too much. Meetings interfere with our regular work and we want them to conclude as rapidly as possible. We barely give ourselves time to think, why should we give it to others? Unless they are trying to avoid real work, I have rarely seen people enthusiastically look at their schedule for the day and proclaim their gratefulness for the meetings scheduled.

The plethora of ineffective business meetings sparked a focus on tight structure and effective meeting conduct—specific agendas with time limits to each item and facilitator roles to keep the meeting moving forward. Unfortunately, the way we organize meetings can provide serious detriments to thinking. Meetings have time constraints but thinking has no time limit and does not appear at the demand of the clock. Few facilitators have the training to track the thinking of different people, allowing thoughts to flow in different directions and then helping to bring all of it together.

As we have sought to increase the efficiency of meetings in response to the widespread disdain for them, we have not moved one inch closer to effective meetings that move collective thinking beyond existing boundaries. If you have had that experience, be thankful, it is rare. Meetings need limits. We do not want repetition of ideas and rehashing of the same thoughts. The fear of this annoying state when people are debating different opinions pushes us into restraining any process that seems to be taking too long, but the agenda-facilitator-time budget method will not work when thinking is valuable. You cannot create strategy through boundaries on thinking. You cannot create strategy through haphazard thinking or combative thinking. Collective thinking requires a higher level of skill than conducting an effective traditional meeting.

To the extent that we ask people to share their thoughts at meetings, we more often fall into various traps. Sometimes the meeting resembles talk radio with everyone clamoring for a platform to express their opinions. No one is really listening to any one else, so there is no possibility for thinking to become beneficially intertwined. In other circumstances, the meeting resembles TV pundit discussions with the participants debating from preformed decisions trying to win. People are listening only to find gaps in the other person's ideas, so there is no collective building of thought to new frontiers. In other circumstances the meeting leader is striving for *buy-in*, so the attendees are taken through some spurious process to direct their thinking toward the desired conclusions. People listen to figure out how to appear to be on board, stifling questions or thoughts that deviate from the obvious path. In other circumstances, people remember that every act of theirs is being evaluated and fed into their performance appraisal so they find ways to participate to look smart. People listen for their opportunity to speak and demonstrate their knowledge; they do not ask questions. Finally, there is the most feared meeting of all—something has gone wrong and it's time to fix it. This is the time when we invoke our repertoire of scatological references to describe the situation and our reaction to it. No time for thinking, everyone is trying to figure out how to cover their a—-s.

The Sound of Many Minds Thinking

The major focus of this book is a variety of thinking processes you can use individually or collectively when facing strategic decisions. Each of these processes has a similar structure of expanding thought outward to include a variety of ideas and perspectives, exploring new terrain, and coalescing thought toward some conclusion. Allow me to give you some basic ideas for bringing more focused thought into a meeting; then I want to turn to the more challenging issue of building toward collective thought.

- Use the strategic thinking processes in this book to organize a meeting rather than an agenda of items to accomplish.
- Alternatively, consider creating a meeting structure by developing a series of thought-provoking questions for the group.
- Ensure that there is sincere effort to understand each other's thinking rather than defending one's own ideas.
- Push to explore thinking and ideas.
- Have patience for the answering process evoked by the questions.
- Have confidence that you will arrive at insightful answers.
- Schedule another meeting to continue the thinking process rather than having thinking stop because you ran out of time.

When we come together to think we face many restraints. Let's push the time restraints away. Using some of the points in the list above—there is no agenda with multiple items and a time schedule for each item. The only item for the meeting is the one subject for the focus of thought; it can be a large, complex subject but there will be no pressure to move from one point to the other. It is crucial to drop the restraint imposed by needing to come to a final decision, although it is always valuable to move from expansive phases where ideas are being generated and thinking is moving outward to contracting phases where there is some momentary evaluation of what is important or central and some tentative conclusions emerge. The key is to keep these transient evaluations and conclusions from rigidifying further thought.

Whenever people come together in a business meeting, many of the old issues return, including all the negative experiences of past meetings. There are issues of trust, hierarchy, experience with the topic, experience with different people in the room, preformed judgments, career concerns, and so forth. In addition to these biases, we have our mixture of feelings about group processes. All these issues, including the restraints of time, are important to the success of a thinking meeting. I am choosing not to address them. Taking the privilege accorded to all scientists, I assume those problems do not exist, so we can focus on the challenging aspects of moving individuals to a healthy state of collective thought. Inevitably, the neglected issues intertwine with these aspects but I am leaving them in the background so we can continue to explore the arena of thought.

As the word *meeting* carries relatively negative connotations from experience, it has become more popular to refer to thinking get-togethers as *dialogues*. It is a good choice, as the dictionary gives us the definition *interchange and discussion of ideas, especially when open and frank, as in seeking mutual understanding and harmony*. The Greek roots *dia*, between, and *logos*, word, create this deeper sense of conversation as the word *logos* has several meanings—*the word, the word by which the inward thought is expressed, and the inward thought itself*. Clearly, this sets a standard for group get-togethers that is different from our customary experience. It is not, however, out of reach. David Bohm (*Unfolding Meaning* and

On Dialogue) has interesting work on dialogue. I am going to explore a few different stages in a group striving to reach this level of collective thought and make some comments about individuals and the facilitator role for each stage. Do not consider these stages as absolutely and always sequential in time.

What happens when people first come together to share their thinking? When our topic is business strategy, we should expect that people are coming with prior thought and knowledge. They have different perspectives and experience with the topic. They're intelligent people, so they have probably been thinking about it. People probably have formed some ideas about the topic. They're different people, so they probably have divergent ways of thinking about things and the topic in particular. People differ in their thinking in terms of what they choose to emphasize or where they begin to focus their attention. For example, marketing, production, and finance people clearly have different ways of thinking about things. With any kind of luck, people really care about the topic and their stake in it. Why would we want people thinking about something for which they experienced no true responsibility?

An article on strategy in *The Economist*, March 1, 1997, picked up on this need for different perspectives by summarizing some of Gary Hamel's ideas for generating strategy. He suggests using more outsiders such as new recruits or people away from the head office, opening perspectives to new ways of thinking, and ensuring more passion for the topic by having people with a stake in implementing strategy.

The key point, however, in a group process should be the ability to move to different perspectives. For example, suppose you take a group of people to a busy street corner and ask them what they observe. It is unlikely they will have the same report. Each person will tend to emphasize some things over others, bring some things to the foreground, ignore other things, and have personal priorities and interests. You can see how varied these perspectives can be by imagining being at a street corner and considering different questions. What are the shopping patterns? The traffic patterns? How do people relate to each other when they are walking together? How do people respond to or ignore strangers? What kinds of people pass by this street corner? Where are the possibilities for improvement? Each question provokes another perspective and line of thought.

Similarly, in this first stage of a group striving for collective thought, even if all the other typical group problems have floated away and everyone attends with the best of intentions, we still have mental chaos. People are on different wavelengths. Thought is traveling in different directions. If everybody already had the same thoughts and perspectives, why bring them together? What do we gain if we all think alike? We can't patch up the differences; we don't want to. We want to bring them out; they do not separate the group but provide the fuel for moving beyond what people currently know. The purpose of thinking together is to encourage people collectively to break the bonds of their own paradigms, their own volunteered slavery, and move to new thoughts. The different perspectives are valid because they form different images of the whole we are trying to grasp. The presumption is that we could not get where we are heading on our own because we have only one piece of the puzzle. It is similar to a treasure hunt in which each participant has only one clue and the participants need to work together to succeed. The job of each participant is attentiveness to the ideas of others without feeling a need to defend one's own positions, or in the spirit of teamwork, suppressing one's thoughts for the harmony of the whole. In terms of thought, this is not harmony but politeness inhibiting progress. The facilitator's role is drawing the differences to the surface in unambiguous terms. The purpose is not to push the group apart or find any resolution but to establish the ground from which the group can move forward. That ground consists of what the group knows and is collectively thinking.

The second stage occurs quite frequently among well-meaning people—all ideas are equally valid as all have a version of truth.

> The first word 'Ahhhhhh'
> blossoms into all others.
> Each of them is true.
>
> KUKEI, *Singing Images of Fire* (Jane Hershfield, translator)

There is a wonderful spirit of cooperation in this experience. It is a worthy intermediate stage. We have the initial ideas out without killing any of them. The job of the participants is to enjoy the stage without allowing it to lull them to sleep in the belief that this kind of agreement completes the work. This is strategic thinking. We are driving not toward one truth but toward a direction to follow to which everyone can become committed. In this stage, all paths look great. When we are alert, we realize that the world offers us numerous possibilities; our task is choosing among them. The facilitator's role is translating the power of this feeling among people to other stages. In the first stage the facilitator may have been working with the natural human tendency to evaluate and see things as right or wrong. This is the stage in which people have moved past that and have the natural stopping point of dropping all evaluation. Thinking requires judgment but it has a different quality as it reappears in the next few stages.

In the first stage we brought the differences to the surface and then came to the point at which everything was nearly equivalent. In this third stage we push deeper—to the meaning and origins of the ideas. Why do people think what they do? Be careful, the question, *why do you think that?*, with the wrong emphasis on *why* and *that,* challenges with the idea of destroying. We want to know the source of people's thinking, what led them to what they are saying, what assumptions they may be making, why it is important to them. The job of each participant is to allow those assumptions and paradigms to surface along with the meaning and reasoning for the ideas. Where people had reasonable confidence, some self-doubt might enter. It is not about being wrong but about noticing that the foundation may be a little shaky.

The facilitator's role is emphasizing the naturalness of this stage. People formed ideas on the basis of their perspectives. They needed assumptions and paradigms to make sense of a complex world. They created order with a partial view or their own experience. Simultaneously, they were focusing on things they felt important. People's values play a major role in how they think about things. The facilitator may focus on these values, certainly not to change them, but to connect them in everybody's views to the kinds of ideas people represent. If we have values present, we have people working with something they care about. It seems to me that this third stage is the first one in which serious thinking enters; up to this point we have had honest discussion. In addition, the last two stages are not reachable if participants do not have some type of passion for the topic.

The fourth stage is the door to inquiry—asking each other real questions. It is challenging each other to move to new understanding or new ideas, not to find fault. The job of each participant is to have a spirit of inquiry—willing to be questioned and say *I don't know.* People need to ask *dumb* questions. *We've been talking for a while about (efficiency, improvement, quality, etc.); what do we mean in this business or context?* This kind of question, rather than testing people, frequently moves them to a new level of understanding. The facilitator's role is to be right in the fray, asking questions and ensuring that all inquiry is helping individuals to increase their level of understanding and insight rather than just responding with what they already know.

We come to the fifth stage—where we have arrived at collective thought. There is a difference between group-think and collective thought or dialogue. In group-think, everyone thinks the same thing; we are homogenized clones of each other. We *buy in* and *get with the program.* The experience of collective thought at this stage is quite different. Group-think feels restrictive—your mind is forced to participate with the group. Collective thought feels liberating—your mind is with the group. I could call it magic or some elevated energy state but it occurs at the moment at which the thinking is among the people and thought is moving through the room connecting everyone to it. In some sense, thought is outside, rather than within an individual. Individual thinking accelerates by being part of the discussion rather than isolated from it. Through participation it is possible to reach insight unreachable on one's own. The job of each individual is to stay connected to the flow of thought and participate in the facilitator role, because at this point you do not want the facilitator being an outside observer trying to help the group. The shared facilitator's role is keeping the thread of thinking moving forward. Regardless of the quality of the discussion, the possibility always exists for any individual to fall into mental chaos or lapses through not understanding, being tired, or, when hearing something provocative, falling into internal thought processing, separate from the group. The nature of understanding, harmony, or cooperation among the group is at a very different level. Everyone has moved into the flow of thought as it moves into new terrain toward its conclusions by using what they know but not being restrained by it.

CHAPTER 5

More Than You'll Ever Know

I refuse to be intimidated by reality anymore. After all, what is reality anyway? Nothin' but a collective hunch. Reality is the leading cause of stress amongst those in touch with it.

JANE WAGNER,
The Search for Signs of Intelligent Life in the Universe

We expect information to tell us the truth about reality. Even if we could fully trust quantified data, believing it to be completely objective, untouched by human interpretation or manipulation, we would have insufficient insight into the world around us. This form of information, despite its voluminous existence, is only a small piece of the puzzle. Once we move into other forms of information we enter the subjective world of human interpretation. Regardless of its form, there is no end to information as there is no end to what we could know about something. How much do you know about your customers or competitors? When would you ever stop learning? Each day as you are gathering information, something else happens and then you have to gather information on that. As in *Alice in Wonderland, you are running faster and faster to stay in place.* You could make a career of gathering information and never make a decision about anything. We certainly want information on customers and competitors, as Larry Kanaher writes in his book *Competitive Intelligence.* Past behavior may reveal patterns, but we really want to know what people will do and what they are thinking.

It is a joke that reflects common experience to say, *let's form a committee.* This is such a frequent response to the query—*what should we do about x?*—that we have to wonder what we really expect to learn. Why don't we decide right now? Why do we need to gather more information? Often information gathering is a barely disguised way of avoiding thinking and decisions. There is more information about the past and the present than we could ever gather and use. There is no information about the future, the terrain of strategy. No matter how much information we gather, we can never completely remove uncertainty about the future. We have a paradox. Thinking requires a knowledge base that depends upon access to information. Thinking is necessary to arrive at the decisions that lead us to act. If you are going to wait to act until you have *complete* or *perfect* information, the time to act will long pass you by. If you are going to act with minimal information, you might as well throw a dart because your decisions will border on randomness, involving little thought. What is the right amount of information? We need to think about the value of information to the organization so that the search is not wasteful of time or money.

The driving energy should be the quest for information that helps respond to real questions (Chapter 3) or moves the quality of collective thought (Chapter 4) toward the strategy. We often have trouble accurately recollecting the past, we frequently have quite different perceptions from each other about the reality of the present, and we can never know the future with certainty. Therefore, the only value of additional information is that it has some reasonable chance of altering the decision we would make with the information we have right now. It should open thinking to opportunities we are unable to see or to threats we may be overlooking. Otherwise, we waste time, money, and energy. If the drive to seek more information derives from reluctance to commit resources to an existing decision, then the only thing attained by continuing the search for information is a delay of action rather than a building of knowledge. If there is no possibility of altering a decision or seeing something new, the only value of new information would be to affirm what we would already do. Affirmation may add to a sense of security—there is nothing wrong with more restful sleep—but the organization must question whether it really needs to invest in the expense of further information for that feeling.

The following six steps are a useful way to think about information:

- Accepted information
- Interpretations
- Evaluations
- Tentative business decisions
- Assessing the need for new information
- Choosing methods to obtain desired information

It is useful to follow these steps in the order given. Think of it as an ongoing flow through the steps until the tentative business decision becomes the chosen direction. Until that point, new information is a strong possibility. There is also a feedback loop from the last step—*choosing methods to obtain desired information*—to the first step—*accepted information*. As we move through a discussion of the flow and feedback in the six steps, consider them completely applicable to the work of an individual, a group, or coordinated efforts throughout the organization.

The first step, *accepted information*, reveals the current state of the knowledge base. This needs to be relatively objective. Verifiable quantified data is a common category—market shares, income levels, demographics, financial information, sales levels, and so forth. It should also include descriptive information obtained through observation or experience. For example, salespeople through their contacts with customers possess significant information.

Accepted information contains anything that results from previously used methods of information gathering—publications, surveys, interviews, informal discussions, and so on. Given the nature of the feedback loop, it is quite easy in this step to assess the worth of the last round of information gathering. *Did the methods previously chosen add to information? Do we have more data or more knowledge? Do we have more insight about the topic or issue?*

The information reflects the past and the present. It does not relate to the future, as we get our sense of the future only by going through the next two steps—*interpretation and evaluations.* In this first step, therefore, we are trying to be as objective and accurate as possible in creating a clear view of the information, unfiltered by our subjective interpretations and evaluations.

The second step, *interpretations*, illuminates our subjectivity. It is a challenge to separate our filters, biases, and interpretations from the information itself. The first step established a ground upon which everyone can agree. It does not mean that everybody knows everything. That would be impossible and a terrible waste in duplicating efforts. Agreement means that anyone who knew the information would see the same thing. As soon as they see something different from each other, they are moving into interpretations. Different paradigms drive interpretations. The world also looks very different from different jobs within the organization. The significance of any event or information also shifts. For example, everyone in the organization may see that sales are declining, but the evaluation of the sales department may be that product development has not matched pace with the evolution of the market or that production has been unable to restrain costs. The evaluation of the production department could be that salespeople have paid insufficient attention to customer needs.

Trying to determine why something happened or the significance of something will inevitably involve our perspectives. These different perspectives are valuable in activities of collective thought (Chapter 4). If everyone knows the same thing and thinks the same way about it, there is redundancy. We have another paradox regarding information—we want to have different perspectives, but these perspectives cause us to take the same *accepted information* and arrive at different *evaluations*. Therefore, it is important in this stage for everyone to recognize that these perspectives will filter the data and lead inevitably to different interpretations. From these different interpretations, different evaluations will flow. By directly addressing these interpretations—understanding them but not necessarily resolving them—people move through the other steps of thinking about information in a relatively cohesive fashion. Pushing the interpretations aside will magnify problems. People will battle over the business decisions, the need for new information, or the best way to gather new information. If there is no way to come to an agreement, people will hunt for information that confirms their belief.

There is another other facet of interpretation worth mentioning—different attitudes toward risk. Business decisions always have uncertainty; information can reduce it but never fully remove it. For example, anything that has had a history of fluctuations in the past—oil prices, inflation rates, stock market valuations—will lead people with a lower tolerance for risk to view the instability as detrimental and likely to continue. This attitude could lead to a desire to delay a decision, make it more conservative, or try to get more information to better understand the fluctuations. A person with a higher tolerance for risk will see manageable conditions ahead. This person could be willing to make a decision, perhaps one that is less conservative, and be less likely to pursue additional information.

Finally, interpretations are important because it doesn't always matter how people inside the organization think about the information. If sales are declining, the customers' interpretations of the data may be more informative than those of the sales or production department.

The third step, *evaluations*, helps determine why things happened the way they did, what is likely to happen in the future, the relative significance of different information, and the assumptions we need to make. Let's deal with these four issues in order.

The determination of why things happened is an attempt to get at cause and effect or underlying reasons to really understand the past. Information tells what happened; intelligence uncovers the *why*. Frequently, the future is simply an extension of the past with trends projected from the information. With deeper understanding about why things occurred the way they did, it is possible to see if the future will be a significant departure from the past.

There is much more information available than it would be desirable to know. Therefore, we must constantly push our thinking out to encompass a widening net of this information and then make choices to focus on items we consider significant or essential. We can never reach this judgment if we begin with a narrow focus. We need to see what is available and choose from it by assessing the relative significance of different information.

It is easy to see that people with a high tolerance for risk are probably likely to tolerate a greater number of assumptions than people with a lower tolerance for risk; they are also more likely to make assumptions on sketchier data. Assumptions are the main way we address uncertainty. We do not know what is going to happen, we have information that will give us some idea, and then we make assumptions to help us come to a decision.

In the fourth step—*tentative business decisions*—the basic question is, *given what we now know, what would we choose to do*? We must make this step to help focus the drive for new information in the next two steps. We assess our degree of comfort with a decision, attitude toward remaining uncertainty, and confidence in assumptions. *Could our minds be easily shifted to a different decision alternative?* I think our bias should always be toward exiting the process at this point and sticking with a decision. Any decision, even a tentative one, follows from careful thought through the first three steps and then challenging work to understand the alternatives and choose the one that seems best. We want to restrain our desire to get new information and delay decisions. Every thinking process in this book has an explicit focus on conclusions. Thinking is targeted toward action—either making a decision and implementing it or needing new information, getting it, and moving toward a final decision.

Entering the fifth step—*assessing the need for new information*—means we lack confidence in the decision because we cannot handle the uncertainty and think the assumptions are quite tenuous. When the mood is, *if we only knew these specific issues with greater clarity we would be in a better position to decide*, it is a good idea to continue the information process. Regardless of the level of comfort with the tentative decision, there is no value in new information if we cannot gain clarity on several *what if* questions. We are mentally testing the consequences of different things the new information could reveal. *What if we found out _____, how would we change the decision?* When the decision flickers easily with the slightest change in wind, it may be wise to delay the decision and continue the search. This step clarifies the new information worth knowing.

The final step—*choosing methods to obtain desired information*—looks at whether the new information worth knowing is knowable. Maybe more information on consumer demand would help the choice of some product characteristic. Where is that information available? How is it obtained? It is possible that there is no viable method for obtaining the desired information. This is not prediction of the future, consumer demand in this case, but speculation on the availability of new information and its possibility of revealing more insight about the future. Even if there is a viable method, it becomes necessary to assess the time and cost involved in pursuing this method. Even if all this analysis leads to a go ahead on new information, the process needs ongoing checks. If the new information is not altering the current knowledge base in a way that will seriously influence the business decision, the search should be stopped.

Information is important, but why waste time getting more if our thinking can effectively use what we already know? This effectiveness depends upon the quality of questions and collective thought. It is significantly less expensive and less time consuming to focus on one's abilities in these two areas than to rely on more information to resolve the problem. Once we have more information, we still face the issue of how we think about it.

CHAPTER 6

The Opposing Forces of Thought

I am the rest between two notes, which are somehow always in discord.
RAINER MARIA RILKE, *Selected Poems* (Robert Bly, translator)

The Mind's Two Notes

Logic versus intuition. Synthesis versus analysis. Convergence versus divergence. Holistic versus divided. Sequential versus simultaneous. Hierarchy versus network. We have many ways of describing the battles engaged within our minds. Each pair describes contrasting thought modes. It is a curious facet of our attitudes that we often transform *contrasting* to *conflicting* and wind up believing one must be better than the other. We customarily approach issues as right or wrong, good or bad, success or failure. For thinking we need to move from polarity to complementarity. Especially in a society that tends to favor heavily logic, analysis, convergence, divided, sequential, and hierarchical, we need to break the chains of this destructive dualistic belief. I am not talking about some mushy harmony where everything blends. The power for thinking comes from the distinctive nature of each side of the pairs. Think of these pairs as breathing; inhaling and exhaling are different processes. Both are necessary but they are always in discord. We do only one at a time; we can't do them simultaneously—unless, of course, you're playing the didgeridoo and using circular breathing. They're not in opposition, however; the value of each depends upon doing the other one correctly. This example may seem a little trite, but high-altitude mountaineers have learned that the best way to breathe is to exhale heavily, creating a vacuum so that the inhalation can pull in more oxygen in the thin air. They do not force the inhalation. I think it's the same for these thinking pairs. Improved use of one thought mode depends upon better attention to the complementary mode.

In Chapter 2 we spoke briefly about paradigms and how fundamental they are to our thinking as they form patterns from the past by which we view the present world and contemplate the future. The thought modes in the contrasting pairs capture an even deeper level of the mind. In one thought mode only some paradigms are possible. In the complementary mode, other paradigms are possible. A paradigm can be broad—a belief about how the world operates—or narrow—what is of significance in a specific industry. Paradigms develop from one's experience and knowledge as a way the mind creates order and patterns in the presence of complexity. It is always one goal of thinking to find some way of simplifying reality; paradigms do this. These thought modes are the mechanisms by which a mind processes order and patterns to build paradigms. Paradigms aid thinking by forming order and restrain it by limiting the view to a particular order. Thought modes create the mental orientation for forming paradigms and limit them by relying too heavily on only one mode in a pair. Therefore, a way to break the restraints of paradigms without losing their value could be to develop a contrasting set through balanced use of complementary thought modes.

Parts III through V address many thinking processes useful in acquiring insight and developing foresight about a whole business and its environment, identifying strategic levers for competitive advantage, matching levers with capabilities, choosing a strategy, and making it work. These processes rely upon all the thought modes identified in the pairs. By that nature, the range of thought processes should be an effective mechanism for breaking the paradigms that cause a restricted view of one's business and limit seeing strategic possibilities. It would become cumbersome if each discussion of a thinking process drew all the connections to the underlying thought modes. It is preferable simply to engage with these thinking processes directly as their design relies upon balanced use of one or more of the pairs.

If you have difficulty with a thinking process or are not discovering new ideas, it could be that you are using only one thought mode. In that case try to notice which one dominates and switch to the other. Remember, a thought mode puts you on a path that is absolutely appropriate. It will be incomplete and you may not get the full power from it if you do not also use the complementary thought mode. It is just like breathing with one small exception. With the thought modes we need to use each part of a pair deliberately. It is not an automatic biological function.

It is easy to get a quick feel for the power of these thought modes. Choose an important business issue or problem. Quickly go through each mode and write down thoughts about the chosen subject, that is, a logical thought about the subject, then an intuitive thought, then an analytic thought, and so forth. The order of pairs is not important. From this brief exercise—less than a minute per mode—a fairly insightful, diverse set of thoughts emerges. Although not all thoughts may be distinctive in this quick run through, it does demonstrate the different experience in each thought mode and the possibility of deliberately choosing to switch from one mode to another.

There are overlaps among these thought modes and there are probably other pairs in the universe of possibilities. This smaller, manageable set, however, is a sufficient reference guide for the alternative basic approaches that drive thinking about specific issues. The brief explanations that follow capture a few essential ideas about what each mode is, how it affects thinking, when to move into it, and what happens when it overpowers the complementary mode.

Logic and Intuition

Logic and intuition are probably the dominant pair among these thought modes. Logic relies upon a train of thought in which there is a clear building from what is already known. Without a doubt, this form of reasoning leads to conclusions where it is relatively easy to articulate the mental path followed. It is a powerful process because it is easy to defend one's ideas to others. Inevitably, however, we face gaps in our knowledge about events. For example, it is not possible to know everything about customers, competitors, and so on. We use data that is incomplete. For example, using market research data is a statistical approach to understanding some facet of customer behavior from representative samples. We also have uncertainty about the future. Assumptions, therefore, permeate logic to fill in these gaps. Naturally, in a logic thought mode we can trace the path of thoughts to arrive at the assumptions. Frequently, however, the assumptions flow from the intuitive thought mode.

Intuition is a mode of directly or immediately knowing. It is easier to see in contrast to logic. Intuition has no traceable train of thought. Therefore, to many people it seems as if there is no thinking. People often say, *it feels this way to me*, when they are in an intuitive thought mode. That is why making business decisions with intuition ruling the mind makes many people nervous. This would be an error. Although this is not a perfect difference, logic relies more upon data-based information or knowledge and intuition relies more upon experience-based knowledge. Distrusting intuition is akin to distrusting the knowledge built through experience. We should be as concerned with logic unbalanced by intuition as we are with intuition unbalanced by logic. Unfortunately, we are more willing to displace intuition as it is easier to protect oneself in a failed situation when the logic that led there is relatively unassailable. It is easier to defeat intuition with logic than the reverse.

As with all the other pairs, it is a waste of energy and time to use one mode merely to check on the other. It is certainly convenient when logic and intuition lead us to the same place but just follow different paths to get there. What happens, however, when the complementary modes lead to conflicting ideas? Should we abandon the intuitive insight in favor of logic, or vice versa? It is probably more beneficial to pursue more thinking in both modes to resolve the apparent conflict. Intuition will illuminate a flaw in logic; logic will demonstrate a flaw in intuition. Clearly, logic works best when we need to make extensions in ideas from a known information base. Intuition operates better when we want to make extensions from our experience and when a *leap in imagination* is necessary. Intuition is more likely to provide the creative leap to new terrain, whereas logic is more useful in testing the feasibility of the leap. Logic can never originate a strategy that is a significant departure from the current situation; intuition can. Intuition frequently creates the context for productive logic to operate.

Synthesis and Analysis

The type of question synthesis drives is—*how can I combine these things, or make them fit together, so they form something new*? It is an unending operation of further and further abstraction from the specifics of detail to see how things fit together. Concern moves away from the elements to the system or aggregate, for lack of a better word. It has an exploratory nature, as we do not necessarily know what we will find once we start piecing things together. It is a willingness to work with different things, even ones that seem disparate, to find a way to connect them and then see what seems to be emerging from the combination. I do not think that it is mentally very different from bringing different ingredients together to form a new dish. Every time a team comes together we have this experience of synthesis. If the work is immediately divided by people's talents, we lose what they are collectively able to create. Where would Hewlett be without Packard? Abbott without Costello? We move into this mode whenever we want to gain increased clarity of patterns and relationships, discovering, for example, how economic, political, technological, and social forces collectively influence business conditions. We use this mode when we are trying to blend the path we want to take with the realities of the business in the present moment.

We gradually lose sight of the things we are synthesizing; they become blended into the whole and lose their individuality. Synthesis without analysis leads to inaction or ineffective action, because the management of detail, tasks, and so on, is lost. Synthesis, however, gives us a much better opportunity to understand how relationships among things change over time. It is a dynamic approach that aids imagining possible futures. It is analogous to some large jigsaw puzzle in which the pieces are changing shape until there is some insight into the final shape.

Analysis is nearly the opposite of synthesis—breaking something into its parts to better grasp their function. It is a thought mode whereby we seek further and further detail, driving toward understanding the inner working of anything. Analysis without synthesis is suboptimal as there is no broad view of mutual dependence. We become lost in analytic thinking when we continually subdivide things in our minds, looking at cause-effect connections, and fail to consider more complex interactions. Although we tend to emphasize analysis, it is hard to imagine it operating effectively without synthesis. In synthesis we are trying to grasp major market movements and see a realm for opportunities. It is hard to do this without shifting back and forth with analysis, where there is in-depth study of the different factors that influence each of those movements. Whereas synthesis may help determine how the variety of environmental forces and actions by competitors influences changes in customer demand, analysis helps focus on how each force is changing. For example, if in synthesis, interest rate changes interact with other forces to affect customer demand, analysis will aid understanding the causes of movements in the interest rates. It is equivalent to moving back and forth between seeing the forest and seeing the trees.

Convergence and Divergence

As conclusions, results, and decisions have such high priority, we are frequently in a convergent thought mode. It is visible in meetings when there is some impatience with different viewpoints and there is a drive to closure, getting everyone to agree or buy in. This mode operates when people confront a wide range of data and use some, emphasize others, and ignore part of the data to reach some common point. Divergence happens when there is a common starting point from which people move in different directions. This common starting point is important; otherwise, differences seem chaotic. Maybe the common point is a clear problem definition, shared vision or values, or an accepted base of information. The main idea in divergent thinking, even in individual thinking, is casting a wider net. This expansion can be to gain further information about a variety of things from many sources, to derive new alternatives, or see new opportunities. Convergence is having people scattered through the forest and managing the different paths so that everyone arrives in the same place. Divergence is starting at one point in the forest and having everyone scatter to see what they will find.

It is very easy to see the complementary nature of these two modes. As strategic thinking progresses, there is an ebb and flow between expanding thinking in a variety of directions and then focusing thinking to come to some conclusion, no matter how tentative. From the next focal point, thinking again needs to move into a divergent mode, eventually moving toward another focal point. A major purpose of divergence is to magnify differences among ideas with minimal attempt to keep the different paths connected. We often underemphasize divergence as it seems risky to move farther apart. If ideas are farther apart and people begin to defend their own ideas, we fear we may never bring them together. We work so hard to build effective teamwork that we would rather create no challenge to unity. In individual thinking we fear that we will lose the ability to bring different ideas together and fall into indecisiveness. Those experiences with collective and individual thought generate concern; rather than getting the full benefit of divergent thought—exploring different avenues, turning over different rocks—excessive convergence restrains it to ensure that the exploration does not range too far. Again, we need to trust the power of both modes. Divergence will push thinking to the limits, no matter how dispersed, to reveal the full field in which action can happen. Convergence will take this thinking, regardless of its dispersion, and eventually drive to a conclusion.

Holistic and Divided

The holistic thought mode occurs whenever anyone can see one thing integrated into something larger. We try to do this all the time by having everyone in the organization become fully cognizant of how their work responsibilities contribute to the whole business. A holistic approach is a view of the *big picture*. For effective strategic thinking this thought mode must be in nearly constant use. It would almost seem that there is no room for the divided thought mode—attention to one thing. The holistic mode is more appropriate for the conceptualizing and choosing phases of strategic thinking, whereas the divided mode is more helpful in thinking about making a strategy work. We could probably say that the holistic mode is a better driver for thinking about ideas and possibilities. The divided mode is more appropriate for thinking about doing. The two modes probably reflect the difference between strategic planning and operational planning. In the example of the individual job, the holistic mode is useful for job design— making sure tasks fit the organization's needs. The divided mode is better suited to task definition and scheduling. The holistic mode, by referring to the big picture, tells us why any job is important or why any component of the strategy is necessary. The divided mode tells us what to do within a specific job or how to manage a component of strategy. It would also be appropriate to think of divided thinking forming a bridge or moving us toward tactical thinking rather than the strategic level of the holistic mode.

Sequential and Simultaneous

In the sequential thought mode we focus on one thing following another in a regular arrangement, usually feeling that it is necessary to finish one thing completely before moving onto the next. *Simultaneous* is not a perfect word, as we do not so much think of different things at the same time as leap from one to the next quite rapidly with no need for a specific order. Nothing is finished until everything is finished. In the sequential mode we are searching for orderliness so that we can gain some degree of predictability. It is not cause-and-effect thinking. House construction requires a sequence—the foundation must precede the wall framing, which must precede the roof. There is no causality here. Once the foundation is up, however, there are fewer possibilities for the wall or roof. Each step in a sequence limits the options possible in the next. In designing the house, which is more simultaneous, it is possible to start anywhere—giving thought to one part, then jumping to another.

There is a reasonable sequence in strategic thinking, and the order of chapters in Parts III to V captures this sequence. It is reasonable to think about the

past and present before thinking about the future, about the future before identifying strategic possibilities, about assessing the possibilities before choosing a
direction and then following it. It would be a disaster, however, to stay locked
in the sequence and not allow the mind to wander among the steps. The past
and present certainly influence the future; the sequential mode helps to understand this influence. The present, however, does not predetermine the future,
nor is it a simple trend extension from the present. Sometimes strategy needs to
leap to the place where the business through its work chooses a future. This
requires thinking about the organization's strengths first. As you think about
making the strategy work, new ideas may occur that require you to return to an
earlier step in the sequence and learn more. Chapter 5 was an example of how
we have a sequence in building a knowledge base but do not complete the knowledge base until all the necessary information is in hand. We do not always know
what we need to know about the present until we mentally consider a strategic
choice and the requirements for successfully implementing it. We do not want
the sequence of thought to limit options from one step to the next. It is extremely
useful to have a sequence and keep returning to this mode as a reference to help
organize the thinking that flows from the simultaneous mode. We do not want
the simultaneous mode to be haphazard; we want it to serve as a way of bringing
closure to many things at once.

Hierarchy and Network

This last thought mode pair is similar to the previous pair. Sequence is an order
in time. In the hierarchy mode we think of order in terms of importance. The
simultaneous mode moves among the steps in the sequence without reference
to time. The network thought mode moves among the elements or participants
in the hierarchy without reference to importance. There are so many things to
consider in strategy that is natural to keep thinking, *what are the most important
things and what are the peripheral things requiring less attention?*—this is the hierarchical mode in action. It is a very useful sorting mechanism. There is no way to
make the judgment implied in the hierarchical mode without being in the network mode. Thinking about things, giving them relatively equal importance in
a network of thought, occurs until there is sufficient understanding to enter the
hierarchical mode. This mode provides direction to further strategic thinking efforts. As these efforts reveal new or unexpected information or ideas, it is useful
to reenter the network mode and see how the new thoughts connect to old
thoughts.

Using the Modes

To increase the range of thinking we need to understand how it works. We also
need a way to observe how we are thinking when an issue is in front of us. Using

these modes to observe our own thinking improves our ability to recognize thought modes used by others and better understand their perspectives and ideas. In a meeting devoted to collective thought about strategy it is useful to have a planned thinking process that will move the group forward. Sometimes, when the group is struggling to stay together it is because people are in different thought modes about—have different mental orientations to—the same questions. You can use your understanding about these modes to listen to the way people are talking. Each thought mode has its own vocabulary. For example, in the hierarchy thought mode a person will say things such as, *this is what we should think about first or this is the most important issue.* You do not need everyone in the same mode, but knowing the mode gives you a better chance of appreciating each person's perspective. Yet, there are potential difficulties as complementary modes may seem more oppositional. Imagine some participants being in the divergent thought mode while others are in the convergent one. They would be operating at cross-purposes. Participants trying to operate in the intuitive thought mode can be easily overwhelmed by those using logic. If everyone shifts to the same mode, it does not mean they think the same things. It is merely a way of aligning the direction of thought. Differences in perspectives will remain; you will not lose the power of the experience, knowledge, and insights of people in the group.

CHAPTER 7

Ultimate Alchemy— Transforming Thought into Action

Thought is essentially practical in the sense that but for thought no motion would be an action, no change a progress.

GEORGE SANTAYANA
The Life of Reason: Reason in Common Sense

You'll never plough a field by turning it over in your mind.

IRISH PROVERB

The Elusive Elixir

How many workshops have people attended where they have been fired up by an idea, even been admonished to write down some action steps, only to return to daily work conditions and watch all the intentions fade into the background as work continues? How many teams have climbed ropes, gone rafting, and played games to invigorate team spirit only to find it evaporate in the presence of work pressures? How many books have people read and been captivated by insightful ideas only to find it nearly impossible to implement them? How many task forces have gained excitement through creating a new vision or strategic direction only to find a lukewarm reception by the rest of the business? How many inspirational speeches have entertained and excited people, stretching their imaginations, only to have them rebound to business as usual? How many well-orchestrated business meetings have generated enthusiasm only to have it dampened by the steady drip of daily work details? Of course, there are many success stories, but why is it so difficult to take thought we know to be right, and act upon it?

These experiences may create an acquaintance with good ideas. Regardless of the value of the insight, however, they do not create the experience of using the ideas. It is different to know about something and to know it; nothing is truly known until something is done with it. As my friend likes to ask, *of all things you know, how many do you use?*

In doing tasks over and over again, even to high standards, we may need focused attention but we do not need organized thinking processes. If it is necessary to notice deviations from the standards and take corrective actions, we need only some standard problem-solving techniques. In trying to uphold the status quo, we become less and less relevant to changing conditions as the world drifts away from us. Thinking that successfully leads to action breaks away from the status quo; change is inevitably part of the package. If the workshop, team experiences, books, task forces, or speeches had ideas worthy of following, there is no way that all current activities could possibly match the new insights. It would have been a wasted investment in people's time to merely affirm what people already know and capably do.

I suppose if people had an abundance of free time and empty calendars, they could just add the new thought-inspired actions to their schedules. In most cases, however, to do something new or different, something old must stop or shrink. Everything does not need to change, but something must, or there is no space, time, or energy for our thinking to enter our actions. The status quo has its own inertia that resists the momentum of change incited by new thinking.

Rather than jump on the bandwagon of vilifying everyone for their unseemly resistance to change, let's consider this challenging magic of linking thought to action. After all, most people embrace the change caused by a promotion. Problems with change often stem from the same source as any situation in which thinking disconnects from action—lack of complete thinking in the first place. Action is doing it, not talking about it; it is commonly phrased, *walking the talk*. Complete thinking formulates the direction for action, anticipates the possible restraints to and results of actions, guides actions in the moment, and processes the experience after it happens; it could be phrased, *talking the walk*.

Magic Demands Effort

It should be easy to spot one main incomplete thinking problem in the alchemic translation—the people who do the thinking are often not the same as the people who are responsible for the action. Elaborate attempts to get buy-in frequently center on the results of previous thinking, not the thinking itself. It is possible that the people who are the buy-inees would have thought differently from the buy-iners. It is frequently unwieldy and unnecessary to have everyone part of the original thinking, but if the change is significant enough, there must be an opportunity to think prior to accepting the results of other people's thinking and taking action.

It is a difficult situation. Cloaking the decision and moving people through some process with the objective of reaching the original conclusion is a path to cynicism and distrust. How do we get people thinking when we already know the conclusion? Large business meetings, regardless of the fanfare level to launch the new ideas, are not environments conducive to thinking. They do, however, serve to convey the commitment to the decision. Reversing the decision is not an option; therefore, thinking to evaluate it is disruptive. It may help to replicate some of the thinking used to arrive at the conclusion—for example, from the complementary thought modes in Chapter 6 or the strategic thinking processes in the remainder of the book. This is not an attempt to rationalize the decision but to have people exposed to the knowledge base and depth of thought of the decision-making group. Sometimes this is enough to have relatively complete thinking. If so, action will follow.

When it is not enough, thinking must take place in small groups, using serious questions that allow a wide range and flexibility of thought. It is an interesting experience, as the answer is already known and exposure to the thinking that originally led to that answer is not sufficient to engage people. They need their own thinking. They need to follow the same process as anyone else serious about actualizing the content of their thinking. Here are some steps for complete thinking leading to action. We'll discuss them in more detail in the next section.

- Start with some focus.
- Form an intention.
- Seek alternatives to operate with that intention.
- Make a decision.
- Think through the methods and consequences of taking action.
- Take action and monitor the actions as they occur.
- Think through the experience after it occurs.
- Use the results of that assessment to modify any of the previous steps.

Incomplete thinking occurs when people abandon some of these steps or give them insufficient attention.

Becoming an Alchemist—The Decision

The preceding steps for complete thinking are a different way of addressing the three questions of the Preface meant to illuminate the typical form of a complete thinking process.

What is happening here?—The two steps on initial focus and intention.
What possibilities do we face?—The third step for alternatives.
What are we going to do about it?—The decision step and the remaining steps for
follow-through.

Incomplete thinking is most commonly a result of driving from the initial focus (data, information, knowledge, or a previously made key business decision) to another decision with excessively brief visits to intention, alternatives, or the follow-through. The typical rollout of a new strategy, vision, or corporate direction can only solidify the initial focus—gaining clarity about the decision and the thinking that led to it. Can we wait for everyone to get on board? It may be necessary for people to recognize and accept the fact that their opinions or evaluation of a key business decision may be irrelevant. If you want them truly committed, however, *their* thinking must lead to the action. If we are simply telling people what to do, let's tell them, not waste any more time, give them their performance standards and move on. Other than situations in which we want people following directives, we need to focus on complete thinking. Interestingly, starting from a decision others have made is not different from any serious thinking situation. The initial focus always has boundaries whether it's from a previous decision or the nature of the issue being discussed.

People think better when they care about something; they need to have some stake. Frequently, the various experiences mentioned in this chapter's first paragraph are remarkably effective at intensifying interest and causing people to want sincerely to use the new insight. Without intention—a strong belief in something and the desire to do something about it—there can be no thoughtful action. We can mechanically or fearfully follow someone else's lead. If our heart is not in it, however, there is no reason for the mind to be involved either. Much of what we do aims at increasing the intensity of intention.

Thinking stops, however, when intention alone satisfies us. It stops when we believe that if an idea is strong enough or people gain passion from an experience, they have enough steam to act. This is the New Year's resolution approach to management, promising something that seems meaningful at the moment but lacks sufficient clarity about what to do to fulfill the resolution. I think it reasonable to say that by truly arriving at a decision, not only an intention, action is more likely to follow. Intention must move toward a decision and a decision toward action.

This is a major point: to transform thinking into action, the thinking process must lead to a clear decision that has absolute commitment. A problem can arise when we quickly decide in the spirit of the meeting, speech, book, and so forth. It may not be a decision we really believe. This reveals why it is important to hold back the decision process, not jump to a conclusion in the enthusiasm of the moment. Similarly, the positive feeling of cooperation should not lead to some majority voting or compromise simply for the sake of rapidly arriving at a decision. We must ensure that the thinking of everyone is at the point at which a decision is possible.

Thinking moves toward completion when there is a clear decision. Having control over specific decisions inspires people's thinking. The flip side, of course, is that excessive focus on reaching a conclusion stifles thinking. There are some useful ideas in Chapter 4 on collective thought about managing this overemphasis on coming to a conclusion.

In valuing decisiveness, we want to commit directly to a course of action—the outflow of a decision. What we really need in our thinking is space to contemplate serious alternatives—distinctive practical possibilities—that could fulfill our intention. Is there only one action path given some clear intention? A decision has more force in it, more commitment, when the mind has had a chance to engage with alternatives. Why is this so? Buyer's remorse. It is not even at a conscious level. We feel as if we have been drawn to a decision we wanted in the moment. In the light of the next day, however, we wonder if we have rushed to judgment and failed to consider fully some viable possibilities.

The conditions in the workshop, meeting, or book are controlled. What looks good there may not be good in the presence of the reality of work. This is not a problem for thinking if it is complete. We need to think seriously about alternatives so that it is not time pressure causing us to make a decision. It makes as much sense as taking the first decision that comes along. For example, we usually do not buy the first new car we see. We need to process thinking through real possibilities related to an intention—family vehicle, recreational vehicle, or other. We are often unable to sustain commitment when we haven't had enough time to think about alternatives. Therefore, rushing to a decision because of the passion inspired by the workshop or other experience is not prudent.

Becoming an Alchemist—The Action

With thinking leading to a decision, we know *what* to do, even *why* to do it, but we have not yet thought about *how* to do it. People say creativity is 10% inspiration and 90% perspiration. Thinking about action is certainly not the work itself, but we frequently want to move from decisions to actions with insufficient thought. We need a little perspiration in thinking to mix with the inspiration.

Athletes before a major competition need a certain mental state. We too need mental preparation to act. This is not some mechanical adherence to a decision but becoming mentally alert to remain on course. Commitment matters when we decide; it is significantly more important when we try to live with our decisions. This is not inflexibility but readiness to deal with challenges and diversions that will throw us off course.

Big ideas may need small steps. Part of the problem is striving for idea perfection before any action. We often cannot fully think through all the issues related to *how* to do something. We may need to act in small steps, experiments, or low-risk areas. We monitor these experiences and later think about them to guide the next phase of action until we are ready to make a full commitment to the decision.

The question—*what do we need to do?*—flows from the decision. *In order to make this decision work, what do we need to do?* That line of thought often bounces against a different one—*based on what we are able to do, what should we decide? Should we restrain decisions by the current level of capabilities?* If we did, we could never have the type of breakthrough thinking we truly desire. On the other hand, it is wasteful to pursue ideas that are not realistic. We need to consider how much we want this form of realism—firmly embedded in the present—to restrain the future. Therefore, a reason we do not rush to action from a decision is that we can act now only within the confines of current capability. Timing is important and delay can be costly. Waiting to bring all capability up to speed may cause us to miss the window of opportunity open to our decision. We also do not want to act without preparation. We can plan actions that will not fully expose the vulnerability of newly forming capabilities. We need thinking to plan ways of building the capability required by the decision. If we do *learn by doing*, we must think about acting and developing at the same time.

We want thinking that is *outside the box*. The more creative or novel the departure from the norm, the more challenge it is to bring new ideas into existence. It is the standard creativity problem. There are more experiences with generating new ideas, undoubtedly the easiest part of creativity, than with bringing them to fruition. The world surrounding us lives in the prevailing paradigm. It often puts up resistance to our initiatives. This is not an unwillingness to change but a response to something that is outside the normal frame of reference. It is like living in two worlds—the one that contains the ideas, conclusions, and decisions that we know to be possible and the one around us. It is not a battle against an opposing force but the need to think about the realities confronted by bringing anything different into existence. The world to which we return does not share our enthusiasm. It is easy to have that fragile new idea squashed by the outside world. The workshops and other experiences are constructed environments, designed to support the content. The world does not share that design. We need to spend as much time thinking through carrying ideas into action as generating the ideas in the first place.

PART 2

Strategic Thinking Basics

CHAPTER 8

The Heart of the Matter

There is no permanent absolute unchangeable truth; what we should pursue is the most convenient arrangement of our ideas.

SAMUEL BUTLER, *Note-Books*

Thinking is crucial for developing a viable strategy. The trick in guiding thinking is to create a structure that combines complete thought with the flexibility needed to ensure that it aids insight and the generation of ideas. In this chapter I want to suggest a structure that provides the proper balance by relating thinking to doing with the underlying purpose for the type of thinking and the desired results from the actions. I will make some connections to strategy in this chapter but the main introduction to strategic thinking will take place in Chapter 10.

Thinking and Doing

We are usually in a doing mode in pursuit of results. In marketing there are certain ways of operating—market surveys, demand projections, product placement, sales forecasts, and so forth. Profit, naturally, is always a desired result; other important results include market share and speed of product introduction. In production we use a variety of techniques such as materials and resource planning, inventory control, and quality control. In production, of course, we name all techniques by their initials—PERT, MRP, QC—so we never have to actually use words. Desired results include acceptance or rejection rates and production volume. We could go through every type of work or function in the business and list the various techniques used and the desired results. When we studied these disciplines we learned a range of methods, techniques, or procedures to apply to the typical problems we would face in these professions.

Underlying these ways of operating, we develop a way of thinking about or viewing the world. The same problem viewed by a marketing person will have dimensions or priorities different from those seen through the eyes of a production person. We know the techniques differ among professions. It should not be surprising that the thinking used with these techniques also differs. Customers, competitors, markets, and products permeate marketing thinking. Equipment, technologies, skill levels, time, and costs permeate production thinking.

In the preface I spoke about how the insightful ideas contained in many recent books often become distorted to sustain a focus purely on replicated techniques based upon the ideas. Many organizations institute programs of change that are too heavily targeted on doing something different, rather than thinking in a different way. Even if they move to the thinking level, they often want to replace old ways of thinking rather than add a new thought process to their existing thought capabilities. Reengineering implodes when people use it only as a technique for cost cutting and downsizing. Michael Hammer and James Champy, in their series of books, see it as a profoundly different way of thinking about an organization—seeing it through the few key processes that determine the organization's identity rather than through the organization of different job functions.

I am going to focus on the thinking part of strategy as this is the terrain in which it is possible to derive the greatest competitive advantage. I will downplay the doing parts of strategy—coordinating strategic planning in the company, choosing whom to involve, managing specific techniques to gather information. Figure 8–1 summarizes the relationship of thinking, doing, and results—thinking creates guidance and principles for doing, doing leads to results.

The desired result—coordinating movement of the whole organization toward a vision and achievement of specific short-term and long-term measures of success—serves as an ongoing test to be sure that strategic thinking is on the right track. The framework also has one other element present, which I labeled essence. Essence simply means the heart of something—what the profession or field is always about regardless of the particular thinking process or technique. For example, we could say that marketing is always about matching the value of product offerings with current and emerging customer needs. Production is always about raising the standards in using resources to create the desired products. Reengineering is always about the key processes to which everyone must make a substantive contribution for the success of the organization.

This is a book about strategy in which I intend to offer you a variety of thinking processes to improve the quality of strategic decisions. It is useful to have an essence benchmark as a check on the validity of the thinking process. I will advance the notion that strategy at its heart is always about *positioning for future competitive advantage*.

That is its essence. Any strategic thinking process must reflect this essence. It is the purpose that drives strategy. Although the result of coordinated move-

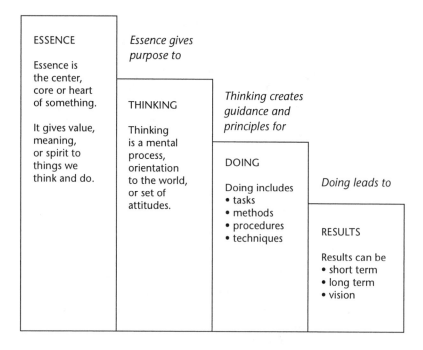

Figure 8–1   The Structure of Any Field or Profession

ment toward a vision measures the success of strategic thinking, essence drives the form and structure of thinking. I am sure that you might have alternative ideas about the essence of strategy. It is important to choose something that encompasses sufficient breadth and focus to design thinking processes that are worth pursuing. I chose these words carefully, and they will influence all the thinking processes that follow in this book.

Positioning

My dictionary defines strategy as being derived from the Greek word *strategos,* meaning *generalship,* and calls it *the science of planning and directing large-scale military operations, specifically, of maneuvering forces into the most advantageous position prior to actual engagement with the enemy.* In war we know the enemy, although we are never fully sure of their potential actions. In business, we may consider our competitors as enemies but the real issue is that we face an ever changing landscape of possibilities and problems—challenges in all its forms. Attaining a static position is not good business strategy. The word *positioning* carries more of the dynamic and changing nature of the environment faced by the business. It is not one position that the business seeks but the ability to alter position as the climate changes and as the business chooses to make changes.

Positioning carries the implication of relativity. There are no absolute stands existing in isolation. In the traditional definition it is relative to the enemy. In the business use we must think of positioning relative to a confluence of various forces (economic, political, social, and technological) and players (customers, competitors, suppliers, strategic partners, etc.) in the environment surrounding the firm. Positioning is relative to the current and potential influences of this complex environment.

Future

Tomorrow. If we think about today, we are doing operational planning or implementing a prior strategy. Strategy must always carry a notion of the future—the one in immediate view, the one on the hazy horizon, and the one that lies beyond. We may be acting now and responding to what we see, but we always need to keep an eye on what could happen or what we want to make happen. The present feels material, it is in our face, but the future is always just beyond our grasp. This is the essence of strategy—to move us to that edge and face the future that we can never know for certain, that requires our willingness to take risk as we make decisions with consequences that we can try to predict but never know.

Competitive

There is no such thing as strategy without competition. There must be a strong force that presses against us to get our thinking into a strategic realm. Every time we think about strategy we are adjusting our ideas to the alternatives faced by others. If there are no alternatives for our customers, we have no need for strategy. Competition is the source of those alternatives. In this vein we can never really understand competition unless we understand the customer's perspective.

Competition does not mean other businesses doing what we are doing but other businesses that provide an alternative way for the customers to achieve the value they are seeking. This is not a simple sports game. We cannot understand competition simply by looking at the other team on the field; we need to understand the changing nature of the field itself. When we see that phenomenon we suddenly understand that competition can take different forms. Did banks anticipate the arrival of AT&T in the credit card market? Customers do not see competition as businesses with similar credentials—banks providing credit cards—they want their needs for credit met.

Strategy requires a sophisticated view of competition. Bill Gates may have a burning push to dominate markets. Is he trying to destroy competition? This seems to be the view of competition as opposition and rivalry. Yet we have numerous cases of competitors cooperating. The more important question is, what does his drive induce in the innovativeness of other companies as well as Microsoft? Once again, the dictionary saves us by giving us a clear view of the meaning of competing. The word is derived from the Latin *competere*, meaning *to strive together*, from the roots *com—together* and *petere—to seek*. The words *competent* and *competency* have the same roots. Whether we are pushing against each other or cooperating, this meaning of competition—striving together—leads to a much better sense of the relentless drive to raise standards and become more competent. It adds punch to the notion of relativeness implied by the word *positioning*.

Advantage

This final word for the essence of strategy almost seems redundant. It is, however, quite important. There must be some dimension in which the business has an advantage over its competitors. Doing as well as they do is not enough for focused strategy. Seeking, creating, and sustaining visible distinctiveness on some market-relevant dimension from the customer's perspective is crucial. There is no way around this in strategy—a need to be better at something than competitors, and that superiority must be more than noticeable. It must make a difference to customers. One of the major premises of this book is that active and fluid use of strategic thinking processes is a capability critical to reaching competitive advantage.

CHAPTER 9

In Search of Process

All our knowledge begins with the senses, proceeds then to understanding, and ends with reason.

IMMANUEL KANT, *Critique of Pure Reason*

What It Is in Thinking

I keep using the term *thinking process*. It would be natural for you to wonder what it is and why it is not sufficient to simply say, *thinking*. When we remember the past, we are thinking. When we appreciate a good meal, painting, or artistic performance, we are thinking. The notion of process gives direction and purpose to thinking. It limits the range of thinking to the kinds that create something new in the mind. Any process, whether it is physical like a production process, chemical like photosynthesis, biological like the circulatory system, or immaterial like a thinking process, has a few critical components:

- There is a sequence or series of steps.
- It is repeatable.
- It has directional flow and is usually irreversible.
- There is a reason for its existence.
- Something is changed.
- It has inputs and outputs with the normal expectation that at least some of the outputs have a higher value than the inputs.
- It has a black box—something happens to transform the inputs into outputs.

Table 9–1   Phases of a thinking process.

Input	Transformation	Output
PERCEIVING	UNDERSTANDING	REASONING
Immersion in material To gain awareness through senses or intuition	Identification and connection of material To know or grasp the meaning, import, or intention	Resolution or response to the material by drawing inferences or conclusions
Developing a knowledge base	Organizing knowledge	Applying knowledge

Armed with this simple understanding of process, I began to consider what a thinking process might look like. What do you think happens when we think with intention or direction? It seems as if it must have something to do with data or information and knowledge. Thinking in some way should transform information into knowledge. We gather information (the input phase), mentally do something to it (the black box), and then have knowledge or, perhaps, a decision.

I pursued the matter further. It must involve intelligence or the development of intelligence. I retreated to the old fallback position in exploratory work and looked in the dictionary. Webster did not fail me. After a few minutes of looking at words I already know, I found the definition of intellect. Intellect is not a function of schooling; *it is the ability to think*. More precisely, according to Webster, it is the ability to *perceive*, *understand*, and *reason*. (The quote from Kant at the start of the chapter describes the same series of steps.) These three words sound suspiciously like reasonable labels for the input, black box, and output phases of a thinking process. Table 9–1 summarizes these three phases with a dictionary definition of each phase and my own thought on what it means in relation to knowledge, the starting point for this search into the specifics of a thinking process. These three phases provide a highly useful underlying structure for any thinking processes, keeping these processes consistent and complete as we approach the different specific mental tools for strategy formation.

I will talk about each of these phases of thinking shortly. First, I want to make some general comments about the phases. It may seem as if this detail makes thinking laborious or takes something simple and makes it complex. The power of thinking, in contrast to any other process, is the ability to move among the phases and treat the process iteratively—making several passes through without feeling the need to complete a phase before moving on. It is not about becoming laborious in thinking but about being free and complete in thinking. The process is working well once it is fluid. There is no need to perfect the input phase, constantly gathering knowledge, before moving on to the next phases. The three phases are as quick as this:

- What do I know?
- What does it mean?
- What am I going to do about it?

We can decide quickly with very limited information. We can implement the decision or realize we need more information, obtain it, and move through the process again. We can follow this procedure over and over again until we have acquired the desired knowledge base, organized it, and have sufficient confidence in our conclusions and decisions. It would be ridiculous to take any challenging issue and believe that a single pass through a thinking process would be sufficient. Those who fear decisions can remain hopelessly entangled in the early phase of the process. Those who crave action can allow their impatience to dominate their thinking and miss important opportunities. The goal of deliberate attention to thinking is to simultaneously increase the pace, breadth, and focus of thought and derail our tendencies to let any form of bias shrink the scope of our thoughts and ideas. We want a rich field to mine for strategy.

The purpose of thinking is not delaying decisions but increasing the likelihood of good decisions. If we are under time pressure to decide, we must move on and shorten the first phase. Remember, however, that thinking is remarkably fast. Although time may limit our ability to gather information, it should never eliminate our use of the whole thought process to think through the information we do possess. We do not want thinking to stop action but to guide it.

A thinking process should feel natural and fluid. Unlike other processes, it may not have a clear demarcation between the different phases. The input phase naturally flows into the transform phase, which in turn naturally flows into the output phase. The line between perceiving and understanding or understanding and reasoning is not a wall but a highly permeable membrane. The purpose of using three phases in thinking is not to force thoughts into proper categories; it is to carry thoughts through a natural progression. It is best for the mind to grasp the entirety of the process and move among the phases rather than concentrate in lock-step fashion on one phase after the other. If a proposed process does not aid your thinking and help you gain new insights, it is not worth pursuing. The purpose of the process is not to categorize thoughts you already have but to organize them in a systematic fashion so that new thoughts can emerge. It should aid intelligence, not stifle it. It should enable us to confront ambiguity and complexity and be able to see a path through them.

Thinking certainly does open us to more complexity. After all, ignorance is bliss. A horse with blinders has very limited vision and few choices. We do not want it to grasp the complexity of its environment and face a wide range of choices. We want it focused on one choice only—move in the direction in which

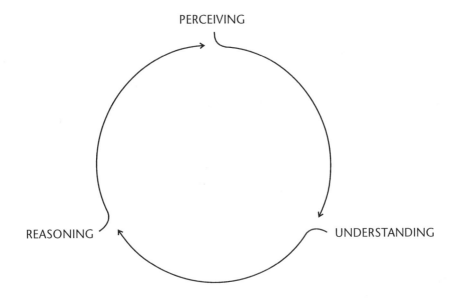

Figure 9–1   Standard Thinking Cycle

the rider or driver points its head. This is no way to develop strategy for a business. We must immerse ourselves in complexity, sticking with thinking to drive it to simplicity and clarity so that the decisions we do make reflect the range of possibilities open to us. Things exist whether they fall within our thinking or not. A retreat from complexity by refusing to think about things is a retreat from reality. It is not practical.

Therefore, it is best to view a thinking process differently from material processes; it is not linear, it is cyclical. It is possible to move to one phase without fully completing thoughts in a previous phase. It is possible to start with the output phase—reasoning—first. Figure 9–1 is a better depiction of a thinking process, showing it as a cycle—with no definite start or finish—and subject to numerous iterations. A circle symbolizes no beginning and no end. Thinking does not have a natural stopping point. It ends when you have a conclusion you choose to live with even if more input, more perceiving, will bring you new and interesting information. There is no obligation in thinking to consider all information potentially available.

Perceiving

Perceiving is an open process that can have no natural boundaries. When does *immersion* end? When have we gained sufficient *awareness*? Strategy magnifies the challenge of these questions. We can never know the future with complete certainty. There is no limit to the amount of information we can gather to develop the necessary knowledge base to help make an adequate decision. After a recent huge drop in the stock market, a financial expert was interviewed about the prospects for the future. Would the market continue to fall, stabilize, or climb back? With 30 years of building a knowledge base, the answer was simple, "If I knew what the stock market was going to do, I would not have to be here early on a Saturday morning answering your questions." This inability to know with certainty did not mean that no decision was possible. If we keep perceiving, we never make an investment decision. If we plunge into the reasoning phase without perceiving, it might as well be a random decision.

How do we know if we are gathering the right information? We can never know the answer to this question by remaining in the perceiving phase of thinking. The terrain for information preceding a strategy decision is enormous—everything that surrounds the business. The only thing that tells us to stop perceiving is movement through the other two phases—what does the information mean and what am I going to do about it? Developing a knowledge base does not mean pursuing any and all possible lines of inquiry. The power of an integrated, flowing thinking process through the three phases is that we can direct our knowledge base development to the areas most pertinent to the issue at hand. In the end, information is worthwhile only if it adds to our insight and has some possibility of shaping our decisions. We can never know this perfectly ahead of time, but cognizance of all three phases will provide relevant focus to the perceiving phase.

Knowledge-creating companies. Learning organizations. Core competencies. Intellectual capital. Each of these wonderful ideas is an acknowledgment of the power of human intelligence as a key component in strategy. Each of these ideas elevates the importance of an evolving knowledge base. In this book we are looking at how we know if we have the proper knowledge base and how we can apply that knowledge to gain insight into the industry, gain foresight about the future, and arrive at innovative strategic decisions. Building the appropriate knowledge base is an important focus of the perceiving phase of a thinking process.

We perceive through two major mechanisms—our senses and our intuition. Sensory perception is quite simply the gathering of data. We can call it fact-based perceiving. Intuition in this setting requires direct involvement in the subject—experience-based perceiving. Intuition is not about subjective opinions of whether something is right or wrong, good or bad. It is dependent upon working experience in the industry. The possibility for intuitive insights builds as one has increasing experience. It is hard to teach someone to have intuition. It is a matter of preventing biases from that experience distorting the signals that intuition can process. It is not idle guessing or speculation but a process whose workings are far less clear than fact-based perceiving. Intuition requires confidence and trust in ourselves and others. It is easy to see why we could shy away from its use and depend solely upon facts and what we call *logical* reasoning.

Intuition works by allowing our experience to process subtle signals from the environment. Send two people out to talk to customers—one who has no background in a business and one who has considerable experience. Assume these are two intelligent people who are not simply trying to prove a point but have a definite spirit of inquiry. If they both ask the same questions and get the same responses, will they return with the same information? I don't think so. There is something about work experience that allows us to see things differently.

There is a small, privately held supermarket chain whose CEO periodically works as a cashier to have direct contact with customers. This is fine recognition that it is not possible to perceive information about customers without direct contact. Data about customers is not sufficient. This CEO, however, is probably working only on sensory data, what he is able to observe directly. It is better than sitting in the office and reading charts but no substitute for the experienced cashiers who spend day after day talking to hundreds of customers, who may have a finely honed intuitive sense from this experience to discern different information from the customer.

I have no way of proving the power of intuition as a perceiving device. Intuition exists whenever we cannot follow a step-by-step line of thought. There is no way to avoid it; intuition pervades all phases of thinking processes. It is especially important in strategic thinking where we cannot rely purely on linear modes of thought. We waste inordinate amounts of time in organizations trying to prove *logically* what we already know. We can never build a completely logical case for the future because we simply do not know. Intuition is necessary to form perceptions and *see* the future.

Understanding

This is the phase that transforms information into its specific meaning. It is the phase of organizing knowledge so that we have something useful to work with. In strategy, this phase identifies key strategic issues, uncovers possibilities for the future, and guides us close to the strategic decision. The complementary pairs of thought modes (Chapter 6) are contrasting approaches to organizing the knowledge base. For example, analysis and synthesis are similar to having a telescope where looking through one end magnifies some portion of data and looking through the other end takes a wider but less detailed view of the whole. Analysis moves us to ever finer detail in the information; synthesis moves us to an ever broader perspective on the whole of the knowledge base.

To understand something fully we must pursue its detail as well as see it in relation to other things. Consider all the phenomena surrounding the business as it moves into the future—customers, competitors, local, national, and international economics, technological change, and so on. To understand fully any part of this environment, detail is necessary. How do we segment customers? What are the salient features of these different market segments? What specific value are customers within these segments pursuing? What are their purchase patterns? There are many more analytical questions like these. On the synthesis side, we want to see customers in relation to the context they face—their role in receiving and delivering value, the offerings of existing and potential competitors and the response of customers to these, the milieu of economic, social, and technological forces that define the lives of the customers, and the evolution of all these connections into the future. Strategic thinking is inundated with balancing analysis and synthesis as well as other complementary thought modes (see Chapter 6).

One way to predict the future is to use analysis and synthesis to grasp cause-and-effect relationships, trying to depict a pattern of consequences of different actions. If one thing happens, what will happen as a result? What influence does one phenomenon have on another? If incomes increase, what will happen to overall levels of consumer spending? As consumer spending changes, how will that affect purchases of the goods sold in our industry? As computer technology changes, how will that affect the design and use of other goods?

If our understanding stops at monitoring effects, we have no ability to predict what will happen. We need to know causes. We need to know how one change causes ripples that lead to other changes. The demand of strategy is the demand of placing our minds into the future. To the extent that the future is a consequence of actions taken today, tracking chains or networks of cause and effect increases our ability to make reasonable assumptions about unfolding events.

Finally, we have the need to determine what is central and peripheral to our understanding. Some of what I have said should hint at the ever expansive, complex, and ambiguous nature of the environment surrounding the business. Each strategic thinking process is an attempt to see this environment from a different perspective, to open our insight and provide the ground for useful ideas. Very rapidly we can face an information overload. I think our mild intuition about being trapped in this quagmire of information has us shy away from true strategic thinking. We need the discipline to move into this morass, armed with the ability to discern between what appears central to our inquiry and what is peripheral that we will ultimately ignore. This is a risky proposition, but there is no other good choice. We would burn out our brain circuits if we tried to consider everything. We would cheat ourselves if we ignored the challenge.

We will be making decisions about what we need to know before we truly know what we need. Therefore, as discussed in Chapter 5, we are constantly called upon in strategic thinking to make assumptions. An assumption is a way of handling the future's uncertainty. The approach is simple on the surface. Something is central if we believe it will have a major impact on the reasoning phase. It is peripheral if it will not.

Reasoning

Quiet meditation and thoughtful contemplation have their place in our lives. Being in peaceful surroundings, going on a retreat, released from responsibility, certainly has some appeal. A thinking process pushes us from this reverie with the demand of the third phase—reasoning. A conclusion. A decision. Thinking with a purpose of choosing a definite course of action. This is the phase of applying knowledge. It is the phase that demands a result from our investment in thinking. I do not mean the impatience that permeates people, runs rampantly in meetings, and artificially shortens the time for thinking. Reasoning is not a rush to judgment but a logical flow from the first two phases.

On the other hand, it is a wonderful idea to challenge oneself constantly, move into this phase, and come to a judgment. Suppose a company is considering a new product, new market, or some other endeavor in which it has very little experience. In an early stage of considering this possibility it may have limited knowledge. Rather than enter a thinking process at all, it often seems logical to create a committee of intelligent people to study the issue further. They will naturally begin an extensive information search to build a knowledge base.

On the other hand, the company is not completely ignorant. Its personnel certainly know more than the average person on the street. Why not push the knowledge currently possessed through the other two phases—what does it mean (understanding) and what would we do (reasoning)? On the basis of what we know now, no matter how limited, what would we do? If we were forced to choose, what would we conclude? Never let the need for additional information stop your movement through all phases of thinking. These three phases are not some cumbersome structure but guidance for a fluid flow of purposeful thought moving several times from knowledge to tentative conclusion until we are prepared to pursue a conclusion and take the risk.

CHAPTER 10

Strategic Thinking Cycle

One thought fills immensity.

WILLIAM BLAKE, *The Marriage of Heaven and Hell*

Planning and Thinking

Strategic planning had its moment in the sun but slipped away under the criticism of the formal processes it engendered. Too many companies had an annual cycle where managers diverted energy from their responsibilities to participate in creating a formal plan that was printed, distributed, and relegated to a drawer or shelf. This is what happens when a perfectly good idea, strategy, becomes a fad and ultimately a lifeless, institutionalized procedure. Many of these exercises in strategic planning became nothing more than operational planning—setting goals for the next year and plans to achieve them, with proper gamesmanship so no one is set up for failure and managers could exceed expectations by a respectable but not ostentatious amount. Strategy is not what people write; it is what people are thinking and collectively understand. Formal writing is useful only as a communication device. It is necessary in starting a new business and seeking external financing.

Planning, typically formalized in written documents, was a one-time event, even if it occurred year after year. It tended to be a highly centralized phenomenon with people with no line responsibilities planning strategies for those who had them. The mind was separated from the body. Strategic planning died when it suddenly became evident—perhaps as competition became global and stability waned—that careful plans could not control the future. Now, however, after pushing some of the limits of reengineering and downsizing, it has become evident that we still need to think about the future. Cost cutting and efficiency improvements have value to the firm but serve as a strategic direction only when the product is nearly a commodity or margins are so squeezed that it is trying to win a war of attrition. Getting lean is a means to an end, not the end itself. It is the way to get the organization in a state of readiness to pursue a strategy. If the restructuring process antagonizes people, their thinking potential may be lost.

The thinking tools in this book will effectively address the necessary approach to strategy—a process that must tap the intelligence that permeates the organization. It must include people who implement strategy in the thinking that leads to the decision; the mind has been rejoined with the body. People cannot effectively implement a strategy they have been handed. The strategy will not unfold exactly as planned—conditions will change. Without participating in the thinking that formulated the strategy, it is very difficult to think about the modifications required by changing conditions. "Strategic planning has been handed over to teams of line and staff managers. . . . Strategic thinking should be seen as an opportunity to transform a corporation and change the rules of an industry to its advantage" (*Business Week*, August 26, 1996).

Thinking is continuous and ongoing, moving with the flow of new information, changing events, and actions by others. The mind is always active. Do we change strategy from day to day? Of course not. There is a huge commitment of resources to implement fully a strategy for a whole business. Although the thinking processes in this book work for strategy within a division, I focus on strategy for the whole business or a whole component of the business—it must deliver value to a customer who has definite, alternative means of satisfying that value. Therefore, strategy is basically betting the farm on who the company is and what it intends to become. It is the chosen direction; other options are deleted. This does not mean it cannot switch completely if the strategy is not working. The thoughtfully chosen strategy could meet a newly emerging blind alley. Although there will be substantial financial and other commitments, this focus on thinking creates the mental flexibility to alter strategy and the business' direction.

The value of strategic thinking is not just this one-time choice of strategy but an ongoing shaping of it, perhaps what you could consider a tactical level of operation. In giving you several different strategic thinking tools, my intent is to aid the overall choice of strategy and the ongoing need for fine-tuning it. We can never anticipate all the possibilities that will appear or all the problems that will arise. Thinking is the critical preparation needed to grasp opportunities before they evaporate and meet threats before they escalate out of control.

Therefore, we need to sustain the thinking process focus as a cyclical, continuous view of the three phases. Figure 10–1 matches the thinking process phases from Figure 9–1 (perceiving, understanding, and reasoning) with the three basic questions about strategy from the Preface. *What seems to be happening? What possibilities do we face? What are we going to do about it?* This connection is a simple summary of the whole natural flow of strategic thinking. It is useful to remember

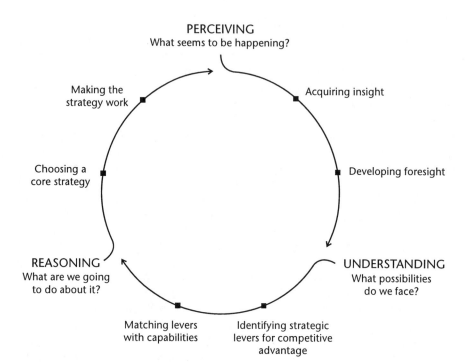

Figure 10-1   Strategic Thinking Cycle

this flow as we add more detail to get the steps involved in answering the three major questions. The cycle has six steps (two for each phase) covering major areas for the full range of strategic thinking. This cycle of thinking lays the groundwork for taking action. The work of information gathering lies outside this cycle. The work of implementing the strategy lies outside this cycle. It is important to see the flow among these steps as one major cycle. In the remainder of the book we are going to investigate specific thinking processes for each of these steps.

Phases and Steps of the Cycle

Perceiving is an expansive process. It has no limit. The question—*what seems to be happening?*—is an obvious perceiving question as there is no limit to the amount of knowledge one can build about the world surrounding the business. It is also a very different thought to try to distinguish the details of what has happened and is currently happening (*acquiring insight*) from what could happen (*developing foresight*). In the perceiving phase we look in depth at the pieces of a puzzle—the various forces and players—and put them all together into a few focused pictures that give us alternative and meaningful views of the future.

This phase of perceiving is more than gathering data; its ultimate purpose is building a knowledge base. It is not the data sitting in the computer system but the knowledge people individually and collectively hold about the environment surrounding the firm. The computer can certainly outpace us in recording what has happened, but we need to apply our own intelligence to give some thought to what could be happening. If you think for a moment about all the things that affect and could be influenced by your strategy—economic, technological, social, and political forces, customers, competitors, related products and services—you realize that the amount of information one could gather on the present (including the past which created it) would tax any computer system. As you try to think about how all these factors can move into the future, it seems to expand without limits.

This lack of limit in the perceiving phase often makes us eager to move to some degree of closure. The understanding phase has much more focus. With the question—*what possibilities do we face?*—we begin a serious effort to pay attention to some things and take the risk of ignoring other things. The two major steps of this phase of the cycle have very different means of focusing. The first—*idenifying strategic levers for competitive advantage*—is the mechanism for determining the most advantageous possibilities for grasping and influencing the evolving nature of the environment. In the next step of the understanding phase—*matching levers with capabilities*—we are taking these opportunities and matching them with the organization's existing and possible strengths. Furthermore, we are looking at the interplay of threats posed by the environment with the weaknesses of the organization as well as determining how the organization can focus upon a few key areas of strengths to form the base for a strategy.

The reasoning phase with the question—*what are we going to do about it?*—should seem like a natural progression of thought initiated by identifying strategic possibilities. The first step—*choosing a core strategy*—is that challenging need to make a decision among all the possibilities. It means following one path and putting the rest aside. It is similar to going to a restaurant with many good choices but being able to eat only one meal. Given a choice, it is natural to think about implementing it—*making the strategy work*.

The Flow of Thought

Clearly, there seems to be a natural progression of thinking starting at the 12:00 point of the cycle and proceeding in a clockwise direction. The power of a thinking cycle is that you do not need to confine your efforts to following the steps in the sequence of the diagram. Jump in anywhere. The cycle's only purpose is ensuring completeness of thought, making sure no stone is left unturned, making sure we do not inadvertently exclude some crucial ideas. For example, you may have an idea for a core strategy (a step in the reasoning phase) without having thought through the other phases. The cycle serves as a convenient check on that idea and you can go through the other steps in any order that suits you. How does your strategic idea match current conditions? Do you possess the appropriate resources and have adequate plans to make that strategy work? Are there other strategic possibilities available? How will a strategy affect future conditions? As you think about a possible choice of a core strategy and what you need to do to make it work, does it alert you to the need to perceive more about present and future conditions?

What people often experience as they work around the cycle is that the strategy emerges. You already know much about your business. It is likely that you have thoughts about where things are heading and how you are likely to respond. If you can keep yourself from growing too attached to your initial ideas, a strategic decision often evolves as you gather more information, gain knowledge, and think about it. It seems more of a shaping of products, services, and strategy, a continual refinement, rather than a choice among several distinct, attractive strategic alternatives. We only experience this type of choice when the selection of one alternative rules out any possibility of other alternatives. Strategy tends to be malleable; we shape it to fit market conditions and our current or desired capabilities. We are keeping our minds open to the full range of possibilities because we want to ensure a best fit and because things we do not do are still open to competitors. The different strategic thinking processes are the mechanisms for this shaping process to create the best fit.

This cycle illustrates the connection among different strategic thinking processes. It is one major *thought filling immensity*—choosing the strategy that is best suited to the environment the organization faces and its ability to carry it out. Given the complexity of this *one thought*, it is senseless to focus on one step to the exclusion of the others. It is a natural process to go through these steps or use them to develop a strategy. Use the diagram to sustain a sense of the full flow of thought in strategic thinking as Parts III to V of this book describe strategic thinking processes for different parts of the cycle. If you look back to the table of contents, you will see how chapters match the steps of the strategic thinking cycle.

You will notice as we investigate these different processes, what I have called mental tools, that it is impossible to isolate one step with no thought given to any other step. As we develop these tools, you will have the flow of thought reinforced. Remember that the aim of these tools is to increase the flow, speed, and completeness of thinking. Remember they are tools; not every strategic job requires the use of every tool. Gain fluency in these tools so that you can choose the ones most appropriate to the situations you face.

Each thinking process gives more focus to a particular area. Although the thinking is all connected, we need to focus on one subject at a time to drive ourselves to the appropriate level of detail. It is not unusual to experience some degree of overlap among processes as they are part of one major strategic thought as captured in the essence statement in Chapter 8—*positioning for future competitive advantage*. Whether you use this essence statement or choose another that better suits you, it should be the core thought for any thinking about strategy. If a thinking process is not contributing to realizing the essence statement, it is not useful.

I designed each thinking process in the other parts of the book to retain the connection to the whole flow of strategic thought—its essence—while you are still focusing on one aspect of it. This cycle of processes is like an ecological system; we can study any component—a tree, plant, or particular animal—but to fully appreciate its significance we need to see it in the larger context. Similarly for the strategic thinking processes—we can isolate them, as we will in the chapters, but it will frequently be necessary to tie one process back to the whole flow of strategic thought. You are only one place on the cycle at a time but with full cognizance of the whole cycle. It will not be unusual in early processes to feel as if you need some of the ideas generated by entering thinking processes later in the cycle. As you work on processes later in the cycle, you will typically be drawing forward some of the ideas generated earlier in the cycle.

Try to use a relatively logical order as defined by the cycle, but this is not about perfecting one part before moving on to the next. It is more akin to watching a photograph develop—a faint outline of the whole picture appears where you can begin to guess at its content, and gradually increasing levels of detail emerge. In a sense, you are working on the whole thing simultaneously, frequently delving into one area for more focus, but it would be too confusing to try to describe the whole thing all the time.

Many of the thinking process topics are relatively traditional, but we are trying to see them in a new light to have thinking open us to new possibilities. It is quite laborious to have a framework that categorizes only existing thought. Ultimately, strategic thinking depends upon what you can hold in your head. The purpose underlying all these processes is to expand that mental capacity.

Figure 10–1, which shows all six phases of the strategic thinking cycle, will appear at the beginning of each part section with the relevant phase highlighted. The reason for this is to be continually aware of the whole cycle of thinking as we work with any one part. There are two or three chapters (distinctive thinking processes) for each phase of the cycle. The individual chapters will also have a similar structure.

Initial Thoughts—an overview to gain some appreciation for the potential benefits of the specific thinking process. A description of the essence of the thought process with some brief ideas on connections to other processes.

Laying the Groundwork (Perceiving)—the thinking process phase that addresses how one builds the relevant knowledge base.

Seeing the Value (Understanding)—the thinking process phase that addresses how one determines the significance or use of the knowledge base.

Moving Forward (Reasoning)—the thinking process phase that addresses useful conclusions or decisions to ensure complete thinking so it is not simply contemplation of an issue but leads to some form of action.

I will usually be addressing implicitly four questions throughout the chapters that you should use to assess the relevance of the thinking process ideas to your own situation.

- Why would I want to know that?
- Why is that important?
- How would that affect things?
- How is this pushing my thinking beyond what I already know?

PART 3

There's Something Happening Here

Acquiring Insight

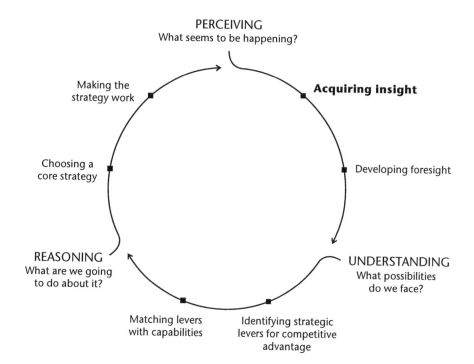

CHAPTER 11

Visualizing the Field

Initial Thoughts

*The essence of this process is comprehending the network of
relationships that define the field in which a business truly operates.*

What industry are you in? Food services, banking, consumer electronics, travel,
steel? Whatever you call your industry, does it help you understand the dynamics
you face in setting a strategy? A key issue in many antitrust cases is the definition
of the industry in which the firm operates. With a tighter boundary, the firm is
more likely to have a large market share and, therefore, a potential monopoly
requiring sanctions. With a looser boundary, it is easier to define a wider range
of competition and, therefore, freedom for the firm to continue on its path. The
stakes are high in these cases, but regardless of the outcome, the industry definition is just a label that may have little relevance for the way the firm should
conceptualize its business for strategic purposes. The ruling on the proposed
Staples and Office Depot merger (*Newsweek*, June 2, 1997) reflects this contro-
versy. The proposed merger would result in 5 percent market share of the whole
office products market but 75 percent market share of the office superstore
market.

By creating an expansive understanding of your business—your organization and the entire context in which it operates—we are moving beyond industry
labels. Frequently, the label chosen for the industry limits our thinking. Just like
any other word, it evokes a system of thought. It can lead to thinking focused
around products (or services) and markets rather than the larger interplay of
chains of customers, clients, and end users; chains of suppliers; competitors and
potential competitors; partnerships or alliances; and complementary products.

In his book *The Death of Competition*, James Moore refers not so much to the death of competitive behavior but to the limitation to our thinking by our traditional ideas of competitors as other firms in our industry. His book is more about the death of industry and the rise of a concept he and others label *business ecosystems*. Whether you like this language or not, it does move us into a different range of thought; it has us spanning several different but related industries.

One of his examples focuses upon Intel. Although it may be rather obvious, it does serve as a good model to notice what happens as you move your thought from a restricted industry label to a wider business view. The thinking process in this chapter will give you a firmer hold on the power of this more expansive view of your organization and its business by visualizing the field in which you truly operate. In the most limited view, Intel is part of the semiconductor industry. This is a multibillion dollar industry where it plays one of the dominant roles, but there are other major competitors who are seeking to push the edge of technology. The many customers for semiconductors probably do not consider themselves part of that industry. Clearly, Intel does not take this limited view, as they advertise to the end users of their customers' products to create a demand-pull for Intel products. It has been such a successful strategy that many buyers of personal computers think more of the chip inside than the manufacturer's label on the outside.

Intel is really part of several industries, and the only way to find a strategy is to understand the relationships among the players in these disparate industries by visualizing the entire field (the business ecosystem in Moore's terms). Intel obviously faces competition from other semiconductor manufacturers; they need to understand these competitors and the moves they are making to alter technology or enter markets, but it is not enough. End users, however, are not really buying semiconductors. If magic would do what they wanted, they would buy magic. Think of all the mechanical devices replaced by electronics—the carburetor by electronic fuel injection, for example—to comprehend the vulnerability that arises when a product-oriented industry definition confines thinking.

If strategy is about the future, then we must have this expansive view to create a base from which the organization can make extensions and to understand the source from which other organizations can act. A simple industry label tends to limit artificially our view of how players can move. Boundaries are a construct of the mind. When we draw boundaries, we often think we have a relatively closed system. This is not reality; it is more open than we desire. The analogy to national parks is easy to see. We can draw borders around national parks but we cannot truly protect the natural resources if we do not exert some degree of management over the entire ecosystem of which the park may be only one part. A business that sees an opportunity or an entrepreneur introducing a new product does not respect our artificial industry definition boundaries any more than nature respects our park boundaries or the migrating herds of Africa respect national boundaries. Certainly, we need to make clear strategic business decisions, but the mantra of this chapter is: expand thinking first and focus later.

We want a wide net to identify strategic possibilities and choose the most productive course for the business.

Laying the Groundwork (Perceiving)

The expansive direction of perceiving is the most significant one for this thought process. You need to drop your thought of the industry you are in. A label may be useful, but choose it after you have created a picture of your whole field. As Moore says, "Start with an understanding of the big picture rather than of products and services. . . . Understand the economic systems around you and find ways to contribute. . . . You must create and defend ecosystem boundaries, building them where none exist, and shoring up those that do."

This part of the process is simple to understand—create a map showing the networks of relationships that directly or indirectly influence a business. We are going to see the big picture, define the field in which the business can contribute, and outline the boundaries. It is as simple as sitting in front of any object, a sandwich, for example, and asking, *how did this get in front of me?* No, not who was in the kitchen making the sandwich, but all the things that had to happen to create the sandwich. Each ingredient has its origins somewhere else—the bread, cheese, tomato, avocado, and mustard (I picked a sandwich I like) have different sources. Things used to create each ingredient are part of the answer to the original question. The whole distribution to move the ingredients from source to point of sale—trucks, petroleum, retail outlets—are part of the answer to the original question. Imagine following the process evoked by this question until you ran out of steam. It is quite obvious that the answer nearly explodes out of control, and before we know it we have the entire planet in action simply to put a sandwich in front of us. This phenomenon of the inclusive nature of the field is similar to the thought (expressed in John Guare's play *Six Degrees of Separation*) that every person has a connection with every other person through a chain of only six people—A knows B who knows C, and so on.

Without questioning the practicality of this exercise, I want you to do something similar for your own business. Rather than put an object at the center of a map and ask how it got in front of you, I want you to put your business at the center of the map and determine the field of players connected to it. You will be getting an ever expanding view of the environment surrounding your business. Think of it this way—we put blinders on a horse to limit its view. The horse can choose only from what it is able to see. If we use a traditional industry label, we are putting similar blinders on ourselves. This mapping process expands our thinking; it has no natural limits because we are throwing the blinders away to have the widest possible view. An expanded view leads to an enlarged range of choice; this is why we want to visualize a field. We want a visible representation of the entire arena in which we operate. Instead of tunnel vision, we want bridge vision—visualizing the links among an expanding number of different players—competitors, suppliers, customers, end users, distributors, and so forth.

Get some large sheets of paper, a lot of blackboard space, or your mind in high gear—you can mentally track this process without writing it down. We are not just making a list but creating an expanding network or spider web of relationships. Visualizing through this business field map is absolutely necessary for a full engagement with many of the thought processes that follow. How can we ever understand value to the customers without seeing the variety of things they see as necessary to accomplish what they are trying to do? We are aiming for a delineation of the multitude of industries that relate to our products. Drop any labels for industries; once we lay out this field, you can choose a term that best represents your business as you find it beneficial to view it. You may even decide you do not need a label at all. Or, you may find the best alternative is to adapt what I call the multitiered industry approach—seeing your business as part of a series of industries ranging from narrowly to broadly defined. As you alter your industry definition, the strategic issues change as you view the map you are about to create. Your emerging strategy may need to accommodate the range of issues that arise from the multitiered industries.

Construct a network of relationships with your product or service at the center point. Start a spider web network by identifying all players (customers, clients, end users, competitors, suppliers, distributors, strategic partners, complementary products) with which your organization has direct contact. These are business relationships representing some transaction involving money, people, information, goods, services, or resources between players. Identify other organizations by name or segment them into relevant groups. Expand the spider web network by adding players that have direct transactions with these other players and, therefore, indirect contact with your organization. Keep expanding this map until the last players added seem absolutely peripheral. Each iteration drives us to a further feeling of abstraction from our own business. Each iteration adds to the complexity of the lines connecting different players. Regardless of how detailed this business field map becomes, it is important to remember its purpose. It creates a broad perspective for fully understanding customers, current and potential competitors, key suppliers, important distributors, current and potential strategic partners, and providers of complementary products or services to customers.

In the sandwich example, the map would certainly identify petroleum companies but it may seem peripheral to what we are trying to understand in order to formulate strategy. Would it help to see the world from the perspective of petroleum companies? It would, if we believe that the cost or availability of fuel has significant influence on the company. How could that matter if we are only talking about sandwiches and ingredients? It could, if the business was a fast food chain selling sandwiches. It could, if the business was a supplier of one of the ingredients and concerned about distribution of its product.

You can see from this approach that specificity, while it certainly increases the complexity, also adds to your understanding of what is really happening in your surroundings. You are not simply defining your industry, regardless of how appropriate you find your label for it. You are continually trying to see the world as others see it. For example, suppose you have identified specific customers—you want to *stand in their shoes* and see the world as they see it. Focus on each participant to expand the map or continue to visualize the field from their perspectives. The world they see contains the different players with which they have direct transactions and indirect contact. To them, your business is only one part of their environment.

I know this method of perceiving may seem a little strange at first, but this is the approach to creating a wide net from which you can later focus your thinking. This mapping lays the groundwork not only for this phase of the larger cycle—*acquiring insight*—but also for most of the thinking processes to follow. It is useful to your strategic decisions to know the full range of relationships among players that surround your products and services. Ultimately, you want to think about why people want your product, how they intend to use it, and the options they face. You want to know how other businesses in your map operate and what their needs are for their own competitive effectiveness. In the reasoning phase to follow in this chapter we can begin to look at some of the strategic implications of this map.

The business field map requires you to make tentative decisions even though you may not have carried any thinking through any other processes. What is the best way to segment customers? This is a critical strategic question. You need some sense of an answer to this question so that this map has some degree of validity. For example, Intel could name some specific customers and expand from each of these companies to identify the direct transactions they have. A different type of company may have so many customers that they need to group them in a way that makes sense to their business—by the point of purchase, by demographics, by use of the product. It may be useful to do this mapping a few times by experimenting with a variety of segmentation approaches. Do not be surprised if some of the players have more than one of these roles on your map—another company could be a partner to you in some circumstances, a supplier in others, and a competitor in others. It is best to deal with the nature of the relationship and identify the player each time it has a different role. Despite the map's growing complexity, aim for completeness to capture fully your business' field. Using overlays or different colors to represent different roles or different types of relationships may create a more visually accessible map.

Facing complexity and being able to focus in the face of it rather than retreat from it and pretend that it does not exist is the heart of good strategic thinking. The world goes on regardless of what you put on your map. Making it simple by identifying only a few players so you have a neat, simple map where you can easily see the players may seem satisfying, but it is not reality. This mapping process is not making the world complex. It is trying to capture the complexity that does exist; this is a big difference. Strategists do not flee from reality. We want first to see this reality and then decide what to ignore and what to continue to think about. Our choice of ignoring something or paying less attention to it does not make it go away; it just shows a place we are willing to take some risk by limiting the base of our knowledge.

There is a challenging trick here to decide what is peripheral to your understanding of the map. Obviously, as you rule something peripheral to the map you are stating a willingness to take risk. The map tests our capability to consider widely diverging possibilities. Recognize that your capability to think about a wide, complex range of relationships could drive your decision about what to place on the map, what to leave off, and what to ignore eventually. If you want to push the limits of your capability, then push the limits of the map.

Seeing the Value (Understanding)

I hope you have found the mapping phase slightly playful and even humorous as you contemplate the amazing number of relationships that have a connection to your business. It is hard to do the mapping without entering this part of thinking and wondering about the significance of these relationships. The primary question of value is—*what impacts do the players or the relationships among them have on our business?* Remember, all we are doing is describing the field where your business can choose and act upon a strategy—nothing more or less than that. I wager that even for the most peripheral relationships you can mentally trace the links to see how they affect your business and could enter your thinking about a strategy.

Not every link has equal importance to you. Let me suggest a couple of test questions to use on your map to lead you toward a discrimination among the links. Look at each player on the map and try to see the relationships from their perspective.

- What is the most important issue they face?
- What would be of greatest benefit to them?

Even though these are challenging questions requiring some insight, try to sketch out the start of a response. Record some of your key thoughts. Suppose you knew the answer to those two questions for all the players on your map; that would be a fairly deep level of understanding. Just imagine if, given that degree of understanding, you were able to see your business providing a useful contribution to the players. If players drew their maps they would see your business as central to them rather than on the periphery and of relative unimportance to them. You would have a rather strong business position.

On the other hand, the map can also reveal alternatives that each player faces in finding something that will aid the player's resolution of those two questions. Those alternatives begin to reveal the true nature of the competition you could face. Rather than dying, competition is rapidly expanding. It is not confined to the firms selling similar products but extends to a variety of players who have options for strengthening their position on maps. In this large field of your map, even though it is only a snapshot—a rather static picture of relationships—you begin to see the dynamic nature of business. Call it a *business ecosystem* if you desire, but you can see that the value of any single player, yourself included, hinges on the degree to which it influences the evolution of the map so that it contributes to the ability of other players to address the most important issues they face and generate the benefits they desire.

It is particularly useful to gain additional understanding by altering your view of your industry. Take your narrowest definition—usually confined to a strict product or service category such as sport sedans or personal checking accounts. Move through broadening industry definitions, such as automobiles and banking services, until you reach an all-encompassing ecosystem, such as transportation or financial services. You may prefer to see these multitiered industries as a series of concentric spheres, analogous to Chinese ivory carvings, with narrower definitions embedded in broader ones. Regardless of your image you will see that each definition holds a certain truth for your business. Different dynamics come into play and different key strategic issues emerge.

Moving Forward (Reasoning)

At this point I am not asking you even to begin moving toward a strategic decision. Your ability to do that in a useful manner depends upon how well you are able to understand this complex set of relationships from a wide range of players' perspectives. Yet there is some useful reasoning you can do. Draw some conclusions from your clarity about what you know and don't know to identify some significant areas for further learning. *What are the most important things you could learn to aid your understanding of the field, particularly in finding more detailed responses to the two questions in the last section?* Let's remember that right at this moment, given your current state of knowledge, you could run through every strategic thinking process and come to a strategic decision. You want to know where the pursuit of further information will have a significant impact on your knowledge base of the field in which you will set strategy.

If you wish, you could ponder some very tentative strategic implications about how you could improve the success of other businesses, how you could improve the value delivered to customers in satisfying their priorities, how you can continue to sustain competitive advantage, the opportunities that exist for you or others to alter the map, and the possibilities for completely new forms of competition emerging. If key strategic issues emerged from your multitiered industry definitions, you can also identify some tentative strategic response possibilities. You will have a stronger knowledge base after Chapter 13, so treat this reasoning phase as preliminary, a first run through, as the next two chapters will accelerate the degree of detail we can apply to the map.

CHAPTER 12

The Whirling Maze of Forces

Initial Thoughts

The essence of this process is expanding thinking further to discern the environmental forces that influence the players and the relationships among them.

Are you ready to go a little further with your field? Right now you have a map that I would compare to an island floating in an ocean. The ocean is the larger context of environmental forces (economic, technological, social, and political) that influence the behavior of the players in the field. This process views how changes in the ocean affect the island. These forces are mostly beyond the influence of any single organization, although it is quite clear that actions by a major company can influence local economies (the value of an increase in Boeing's business for the Seattle area, for example) and that coordinated activities of many businesses can lead to shifts in the forces (the change in society through mass marketing of computers, for example). Understanding these forces enables you to better anticipate how the needs of different players will change over time. We will return to a more detailed look at the players in Chapter 13. For now, we just want to spend time understanding how to think about the forces.

Once again, we are on a path to expanding our thinking. There are more than enough things to consider in the player relationships identified on your map, but that is not a full picture of reality. We have no choice; to be practical we must address the world as it truly operates. For example, economics (interest rates, income level, unemployment rates, inflation, etc.) plays a major role in individual purchase decisions. If the economy is in a downturn or if interest rates are rising, we are likely to see consumers less willing to make expensive purchases and businesses less willing to invest—they will buy less equipment and facilities. If we want to truly understand the players in our field we need to understand the forces that can have significant effects on their decisions and behavior.

I know this is not the first time you have thought of these issues, but we need to combine the ability to visualize the field, which opens us to new possibilities for redefining our business, with the ability to maintain ongoing vigilance about the world around us. You can quickly see that good strategic thinkers are relatively well informed. They have varied interests, certainly beyond the confines of their industry, that keep them well informed. It does not matter how much information we store in computer systems or we access on the Internet—we can always find what we need. We need our own intelligence tied to this information because we need to apply it to two main issues:

- Where are things heading?
- How is that likely to affect the players and their relationships?

Laying the Groundwork (Perceiving)

There are so many different forces occurring in the world that it would be easy to get lost. Try to identify the forces you think most relevant to your business—the ones you believe most likely to influence the behavior of the various players on your field map. Forces may be relevant to you on local, regional, national, and international levels.

Economic forces include the creation and distribution of wealth and other benefits from production; employment levels; wage rates; income levels; governmental macroeconomic, fiscal, and monetary policies; interest rates; exchange rates; import and export patterns; balance of payments; the degree of freedom in markets; supplies of raw materials and energy; and infrastructure such as transportation and communication systems.

Technological forces are advancements in science, machinery, equipment, and products. Technology is embedded in production processes, in products, in distribution systems for products, and in communication systems among players. As the level of technological development increases or expands, increasing numbers of activities become possible. Technology affects the ways we develop, use, and conserve natural resources. Technological change can take place in any industry and affect players in your field even if your business seems peripherally related.

Social forces reflect the ways that diverse groups of people are able to interact for mutually beneficial purposes. Social forces include demographics (age distributions, families, birth and death rates, population growth, health), ethnic groupings, socioeconomic classes, rural-urban differences, and cultures (values, beliefs, and observable behavioral patterns among different groups of people).

Political forces describe the organization and distribution of power and influence among potentially conflicting interests and claims. These forces include the degree of freedom that people experience in any society, their participation and involvement in public decisions, public pressure groups, laws, and government regulations.

Certainly, there is a large number of forces to track. In this part of thinking we are trying only to identify forces we will monitor and obtain recent information about the past and current state of these forces. This is a challenging task of discrimination; the most obvious forces may not turn out to be as important to us as other forces that we currently downplay or ignore. Should we be paying attention to events in another country? Do technological changes in seemingly unrelated industries have any bearing on us? The situation is difficult; we cannot track everything but we do not want to miss something of importance. There is no easy resolution to this dilemma.

Seeing the Value (Understanding)

We left the last phase of this thinking process with an interesting predicament. For better or worse, it permeates strategic thinking where we are moving toward the future and grappling with the line between what we choose to know and what we need to know. In this phase we work more explicitly with the two key issues I identified at the start of the chapter.

The first thing to do to gain greater understanding of the forces is to see connections among them. I listed these forces separately, but we may be better off if we see them in conjunction with each other. For example, a political change can lead to a change in regulations or public policy that affects the economy. A technology can have an effect on changes in social forces. Although there are no simple, predictable, or repeatable cause-effect relationships, we do benefit from seeing how the forces move together. As you identify different forces that are important to your business, see if you can discover relationships among the forces. If you can find reasonable causes and effects, you may be able to reduce the number of forces you try to track.

I want to suggest a few other things to think about in this phase that may aid understanding about the value of tracking different forces. We want to know where things are heading. We are not alone in this endeavor; there are numerous sources of future prognostication happy to sell their ideas to you. For example, *Business Week* has a column on technology to watch, the *Futurist Society* addresses a wide range of forces, the *Economist Intelligence Unit* tracks unfolding events throughout the world. You not only want to know what someone thinks is going to happen, you want to know why they think that. Understanding the reasons for a prediction will enhance one's ability to connect the future of the force to the players' behaviors and decisions.

You can further enhance this ability to connect forces to your business by trying this playful exercise. *The Economist* is certainly one of the best English language magazines for well-written, wide-ranging coverage of the world—reporting on politics, economics, business, cultural, and other issues in a focused, intelligent way. Using this magazine or something of similar quality, choose an article at random. You can also choose some major current event. We are going to follow the six degrees of separation from the force to our organization. Think of any article you read as reporting on some pebble being dropped in this ocean in which we all float. The waves start to radiate outward and eventually reach us, wherever we are. Some waves are barely noticeable, while others rock the boat. As you read the article, try to get the primary effects; as that (or if that) happens, what does that immediately affect? As events or prospects for peace in the Middle East change, what does that affect—the price of oil, the level of foreign aid, prospects for international terrorism, tourism? We are not talking about your business yet. We are trying to understand the force and its effects. Now go to the secondary effects. For example, if tourism patterns change, where are the benefits and where are the costs? Do other tourist destinations have better or worse possibilities? Does it affect profitability in the airline industry? Keep tracing these effects until they start to impinge on players on your field map.

You may see several series of effects as the waves roll through from peripheral players to central players or you may rapidly see a more direct impact upon your organization. The pebble can fall outside your map, but it will eventually hit a player on your map and roll through to your business. Whatever the starting point, recognize how the time line is operating. You are choosing something happening now and as you trace the series of effects you are essentially moving out into the future.

This type of exercise really sharpens your mental discipline in understanding the significance of a wide range of forces to your business. There are other sources to start the process. For example, John Naisbitt and Patricia Aburdene have made a business of tracking large amounts of many diverse, small bits of information. Seeing patterns among these diverse events and how they converge, they articulate megatrends that they believe have far-ranging impacts. These megatrends essentially represent an interaction among many different forces. You can take one of their megatrends and follow the rolling wave approach in the last paragraph. Faith Popcorn and Lys Marigold in their book *Clicking* also identify trends and provide some analysis of the meaning of the trends. They may also give you some of the primary or secondary effects of a trend in an environmental force.

What kinds of effects are we trying to find? Some markets may open up, whereas others may become more competitive. Some players may see their abilities or outputs becoming more or less valuable. Some players may need to become more effective. Opportunities for new initiatives may arise. Threats to a player's direction may intensify. Customers may change their priorities. New competitors may emerge who can deliver value to satisfy those priorities. You are looking for substantive influences of forces on players that challenge you to reconsider your own direction. This is not a process to find data that justifies a decision you already want to make. This process requires considerable effort; it is ill spent if your aim is rationalizing current thinking. You want to move to new ideas. You want to see if new strategic issues emerge or if your clarity increases for previous issues. You want to test the value of multitiered industry definitions to your strategic thinking.

Moving Forward (Reasoning)

There are three major areas to consider in the reasoning phase:

- The most important forces to your field—these are the ones that seem to have substantial impact on players and, therefore, on your business.
- Areas in which your knowledge seems sparse and more information gathering is necessary—these are forces where you believe that further information will remove the need to make too many assumptions.
- Tentative ideas about strategic direction for your business—these are simply stated possibilities based upon your current state of knowledge and current sense of key strategic issues.

You should treat this reasoning phase as preliminary, as the next chapter aims at considerably more detail on different players and, therefore, a better understanding of the significance of different environmental forces.

CHAPTER 13

Knowing the Players

Initial Thoughts

The essence of this process is deepening knowledge about the players.

If you are trying to sell something, you have customers. If your customers have a choice, you have competitors. These facts seem immutable but the world has changed, lines have blurred about what a particular company is. Any organization can play multiple roles—customer, competitor, partner, provider of complementary products, supplier, or distributor. Companies may move in and out of different roles as the situation demands but there is no haziness about what it means to compete, to be a customer, to be a partner. In the competitor role businesses act like a competitor, not a partner. Therefore, it is necessary to understand the competitive nature of their behavior even if they also play different roles in relation to your business. The focus is not on the particular companies but on understanding each role they play. What do we need to know about them as partners, competitors, or customers? Any player is going to fall into one or more of the six roles described below; these descriptions are rather elementary to ensure that we use the role labels the same way.

Customers buy products or services. Perhaps they incorporate a product into theirs in order to sell something to an end user. There may be a long chain of customers selling to other customers until an end user is reached. Each customer, including the end user, buys something in order to create something else, whether it is something tangible, such as a product or service, or something more intangible, such as status or happiness. The value they receive in buying products or services is measured by their assessment of the contribution to their ability to create whatever they value. Customers set priorities on what they regard as most important in helping them in their endeavors. We think we sell customers products or services, but they really buy value from us. Limiting thinking to products misses the full nature of the transaction. This whole phase of the process that began with the field map and continued through the forces to this focus on players can lose its power if *product* is the only focus of attention. To capture the full scope of a relationship with a customer, we can use the term *customer value package*, which Karl Albrecht defined in his book *The Northbound Train* as "Everything you provide, either tangible or intangible, directly or indirectly, that meets customer needs." This perspective moves us toward deepening knowledge about our customers in a more fitting way for strategic thinking. We want to know the value we must deliver to satisfy the customers' priorities.

Competitors are options the customers have for satisfying their priorities in creating their desired value. It is common to see these competitors as organizations who can take away business from you. The language we use is charged with meaning. The word *competition* evokes a network of thought; we think about competition being fair and unfair, the benefits from it, its relation to human nature, the appropriate political-social institutions to support it, and the nature of conflict with competitors. That view does not seem sufficient. Let's remember the dictionary definition—competition from *competere*, to strive together. There are numerous examples in which competition is the main force that strengthens the market for all. My father worked in a shoe store in Manhattan. On one long city block there were over 60 shoe stores. Their collective presence, although they were competitors, built a market for all participants. People went to 39th Street to buy shoes, knowing that there would be a good selection. Naturally, each store wanted to capture as much business as possible, but years later, when many of the stores had closed, it was much more difficult for the remaining stores to keep their businesses at a sufficient volume. Auto malls and the herding of multiple fast food restaurants, gas stations, and motels at interstate interchanges are examples of the collective benefit of competition. Several companies striving together improve the market for all. Competition helps to build the total market for nearly any product. Bear in mind that from the customers' perspectives a competitor is not only an organization selling relatively similar products but any mechanism by which the customers can receive what they need to create the value they desire. This view pushes us way beyond the confines of our normal approach to competition.

Strategic partners are other companies with whom a business enters an explicit agreement, usually for purposes of blending different capabilities necessary for an effective overall presence in the market. Frequently, these agreements exist among companies who also compete with each other. A July 22, 1996 *Business Week* article stated, "This deepening web of relationships reflects a quiet change in thinking by Japanese and U.S. multinationals in an era when keeping pace with technological change and competing globally have stretched the resources of even the richest companies." They used examples such as Kodak and Fuji Photo collaborating for years on a new photo system and Hewlett-Packard and Canon sharing laser print technology.

Complementary products are anything the customer must buy from a business other than yours in order to enjoy fully the benefits of your products—salad dressing and fresh vegetables, beer and pretzels, compact disks (CDs) and CD players. With complementary products there are no formal partnership agreements. Regardless of the quality of your products, however, you are dependent upon these other companies for the ultimate success of your business.

Suppliers are worth serious thought to the extent that they are responsible for any item critical to the creation of your product. Suppliers include providers of goods, services, materials, equipment, financial capital, and labor, including any relevant institutions for skill development. Focus on suppliers where the relationship seems important to your success.

Distributors buy and resell products without making any substantive changes to the products. You may find it easier to think of them as customers but I think you miss the distinctiveness between behaviors. You work with customers to enhance their ability to use your product to create the value they desire. You work with distributors to enhance their ability to make your product available to customers.

You have already identified the major players in the process of visualizing the field to create the map of Chapter 11. In this thinking process you want to provide a detailed analysis of each player focusing on some key issues:

- Focused descriptions of player characteristics.
- How players respond to the environmental forces they face.
- The needs, issues, and possibilities players face and will face in the future.
- How players determine their own strategies and actions.

In essence, to put some meat on the bones of the map, you use multiple perspectives by assuming the position of any player identified on the map and seeing how they view the world. When we created the map we used the perspective of players to identify additional sets of players with which they had transactions. Now we are perceiving greater detail about each player. Think of your experience being a customer of different products or services and consider what the seller would see or do differently if they took your perspective. As you analyze the present and anticipate the future for the individual players, you must take their perspective to better understand what you will face as you try to create an effective strategy.

Laying the Groundwork (Perceiving)

The perceiving phase calls for the building of a substantial knowledge base. It may seem ideal or unattainable but it addresses issues worth knowing about each player. There is clearly no end to what you may desire to learn about the players—each piece of information increases your ability to anticipate the future and form a strategy that may even influence the evolution of that future. There are clearly limits to what you can learn—time and availability of information. Time bears down upon us relentlessly. No matter how much we learn about the players, there is always something else that seems interesting. We cannot continue to delay the decision until tomorrow when we perfect our knowledge, because perfection is impossible. Tomorrow comes and the window of opportunity closes. Availability is also a major issue. There are certainly myriad sources of information that are publicly accessible. The Internet, for example, is considered a great warehouse of information. You can conduct surveys in which you quantify and statistically analyze the data. There are certainly numerous ethically questionable methods for obtaining information that someone does not want you to have. In the spirit of the value of thinking and dialogue with others, I would like to place a heavy value on talking to people who are thoughtful about their knowledge and extending themselves into the future. Use a wide range of approaches to build your knowledge base in the perceiving phase of this process and deepen your thoughts in the understanding phase of this process. With six different roles for players I want to highlight only some specific, significant considerations in each phase of this thought process. Use the following ideas as a starting point for thinking about the players; identify other things more relevant to your business.

Customers

If you do not have a manageable number of major customers whom you can identify by name, you need to identify groups of customers in a strategically relevant way. You cannot choose a strategy without being clear about your target market, but it is difficult to segment with no thought of strategy. The best approach is to try different approaches—segmenting by factors that influence the purchase decision or factors that help define the value that the customer desires to create from purchase of your product. Who uses your product? What do they typically consider in making their purchase decision? How do they intend to use your product? What are they trying to produce or create for themselves or others? How do environmental forces influence their purchase decision, use of the product, or creation of value? Demographic data on consumers is a frequent approach, but it works only if the data are a relatively accurate depiction of differences in the purchase decision or product use. Once you have relevant segments, you want to focus upon key needs, issues, or problems faced by customers within each segment. Using all the data gathered, you want to identify their priorities because those define the parameters for the value you must deliver to customers.

Competitors

You want to know similar things for traditional and nontraditional types of competitors. Traditional competitors supply similar products or services. From the customers' perspective, nontraditional competitors are other alternatives to satisfy their priorities by delivering the value they seek. Considerations about competitors include how they move toward capturing different market segments, their strengths and weaknesses with respect to these segments, how environment forces influence their actions, their approach to seizing opportunities or facing threats, their relationships with other players (particularly strategic partners), and what makes them attractive from the customer's viewpoint.

Strategic Partners

For specific organizations with which you are likely to seek partnerships to enhance your competitive advantage, you want to know the key elements that make these organizations valuable partners using items such as strategic focus, the quality of their products and services, their position in the market, how they address the competitive dynamics in their industries for their products, and the influence of environment forces on their actions.

Providers of Complementary Products

For organizations not in a strategic partnership with you which supply products that customers need to use your product or service effectively, you want to know their strategic focus, strengths and weaknesses, quality of products and services, position in the market, and the influence of environment forces on their actions.

Suppliers

For suppliers critical to the creation of your product or service, you want to know their strategic focus, strengths and weaknesses, quality of products and services, position in their markets, and the influence of environment forces on their actions. You could also consider factors affecting supply availability and how they have or will perform in times of tight supplies—their access, longstanding contracts with their suppliers or other customers, and availability of reasonable substitutes.

Distributors

For distributors who are necessary to provide your products or services to end customers, you want to know their strategic focus, position in their markets (market coverage, experience, and reputation), how they will potentially affect the availability of your product or service to customers, relationships they have with your competitors, and the influence of environment forces on their actions.

Seeing the Value (Understanding)

The perceiving phase builds a knowledge base from which you can push your understanding to think about how the other players value or react to your presence and how things will change into the future.

Customers

- How do you see the needs, issues, and problems faced by customers in each market segment evolving over the next year, the next five years?
- How do you see their priorities evolving?
- How does delivered value need to evolve to meet these changing priorities?

Competitors

- How are competitors likely to alter strategy?
- How will competitors pursue innovation, change and market influence?
- What competitors, traditional and nontraditional, do you see emerging in the future?
- What opportunities and challenges do you see them facing in entering the market?
- What paths are they likely to pursue for their success?

Strategic Partners

- How are partners likely to alter strategy?
- How will partners pursue innovation, change, and market influence?
- How do they benefit from their relationship with your business?
- What potential sources of conflict might your business face with partners? For example, think about relationships they have with other organizations, different attitudes between your organizations about the evolution of the market, or possible arenas in which your organizations could also become competitors.

Providers of Complementary Products

- How are these providers likely to alter strategy?
- How will these providers pursue innovation, change, and market influence?
- How do they view the value of your business to their sales?
- How are they likely to respond to your strategic initiatives?
- How would they respond if your organization changed its product or service to replace them by incorporating the value they were delivering to customers?
- How could they change their product or service to replace you by incorporating the value your business intends to deliver to customers?

Suppliers

- How are suppliers likely to alter strategy?
- How will suppliers pursue innovation, change, and market influence?
- How do they benefit from your business as a customer?
- What possibilities exist to help them improve their operations, products, or services in ways that will improve your products?
- How would they respond if your organization changed its product or service to replace them by incorporating the value they delivered to you?
- How could they change their product or service to replace you by incorporating the value your business intends to deliver to customers?

Distributors

The questions to better understand distributors are similar to the questions used for suppliers.

The Whole Enchilada

Thinking about all the information you have about the environment—forces and players—for your business:

- What makes current relationships relatively stable?
- What makes current relationships relatively unstable?
- Where is change possible? Consider, for example, realignment of relationships and players moving from one role to another.

Moving Forward (Reasoning)

Given the current state of your knowledge about players, consider the most important things you could learn to aid your understanding of the field. These three chapters in the *acquiring insight* phase of the strategic thinking cycle are the major ones in which the gathering of information is an important component of building a knowledge base. Everything that follows depends upon the extent of this base. The remaining thinking processes depend mostly upon different ways of manipulating information you already possess. These manipulations add to your knowledge, as most thinking involves some degree of transforming information to knowledge.

This is a good point to reconsider the cyclical nature of all thinking. You can go through the processes in Chapters 11 through 13 several times as you reveal gaps in your knowledge and choose to gather additional information. Even if you feel relatively complete with your knowledge base at this point in the strategic thinking cycle, you are likely to find that the remaining processes expose areas for which additional information would be useful, throwing you back to the processes in these three chapters. That is why in strategic thinking—*it isn't over until it's over*. No process is complete until all processes are complete. In particular, until you have a clear strategic direction and resolution to make it happen, you will see gaps in your knowledge base that you can fill with attainable information.

As a second part of this reasoning phase, you are in a better position to reflect on the strategic implications identified in Chapter 11, such as how you could improve the success of other businesses, how you could improve the value delivered to customers in satisfying their priorities, how you can continue to sustain competitive advantage, the opportunities that exist for you or others to alter the map, and the possibilities for completely new forms of competition emerging. You can also gain a better sense of whether the multitiered industry definitions are revealing distinctive key strategic issues and whether this helps you gain clarity or a greater range of strategic response possibilities.

Developing Foresight

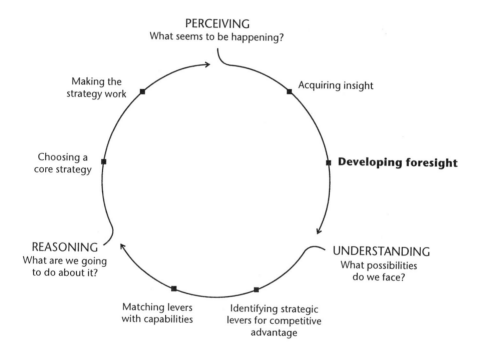

CHAPTER 14

Solving the Puzzle— Detecting Patterns

Initial Thoughts

The essence of this process is gaining ideas about the future by using alternative ways of organizing the knowledge base.

In the last three chapters on the *acquiring insight* portion of the strategic thinking cycle we created the knowledge base. Nearly everything from this point forward builds upon that knowledge base without requiring different data or information searching. As we flow through these remaining processes, however, we will inevitably reveal gaps in knowledge that we may choose to reduce by reentering the earlier work. As different strategic possibilities become visible, we may find that we want to learn more about customers, competitors, or other players to test the feasibility of the possibility or how we would make it work.

Breakthrough thinking on strategy requires creative thinking about the environment. In building the knowledge base through the guidance of the last three chapters there is little danger of remaining within previously held notions as the processes pushed thinking outward. We did not simply look at an industry; we tried to build a network of connections to describe a business in its entirety. We sought to see how different forces influence the behavior of all players connected to the business. We took the perspective of each of these players to get insight into how they view the world and what they consider to be important. Nevertheless, the hazard in all these approaches is remaining within the boundaries of what is known or can be known. In *developing foresight*—in this chapter and the next two—we realize that as we push further toward apprehending the future, we may need to dislodge our thinking.

Chaos reveals the absence of our ability to see patterns. Disorder does not exist; it is only *order* cleverly disguised from our view. Our experience of complexity results from our common misunderstanding of simplicity. We assume it only means fewer things; it can also be many things organized in some clear way. Without patterns things seem random and unpredictable. Patterns exist, whether or not we observe them. Shock waves seem so severe because they disrupt existing patterns, making them no longer viable. Things seem turbulent until new patterns form and stabilize. It may be that shock waves are hardest on those who did not detect patterns in the first place. Those who understand patterns see how the shock waves dislodge them and have a better chance of acting in the presence of change.

Perhaps some patterns in nature are immutable—the phases of the moon, the rising and setting of the sun, the seasons. Most patterns, however, are a result of human activity. They can be deeply entrenched and difficult to alter. They may be difficult to see because we are enmeshed within them and have difficulty gaining a larger time frame or broader perspective to identify them. Our attempts to predict the weather or earthquakes are, in essence, endeavors to find the governing natural patterns. They are not random events. A pattern exists in complex and difficult to observe causal factors. Pattern detection is one of the more powerful thinking processes to make sense of a complex world; it is also one of the most difficult to learn.

The dictionary contains our words, not our language. Memorizing all the words is not sufficient for communication. Language itself is a replicable pattern among words defined by grammatical rules. To understand a language never heard before, we need to know the pattern. During World War II, U.S. Armed Forces used Navajo speakers; the pattern was never decoded. Language or secret code is just gibberish to us until we decipher a pattern. The order is there all the time, just unknown to us when we fail to detect the pattern.

The only way ever to solve the horrendous traffic problems plaguing the country is to understand patterns. Obviously, rush hours, weekends, and holidays create different traffic patterns. These overall patterns help define the nature of the problem. We can partially alleviate this situation when we detect the smaller scale patterns that occur when vehicles enter or leave the freeway. These patterns accentuate the road congestion. Special lanes for exiting and entering as well as traffic signals at entrances are ways to manage these problems.

Many stock market analysts are hard at work trying to find the quantitative model that reflects patterns in stock price variations. Stock market valuation captures movements in global and national economies, the ascent and descent of different industries, the fortunes of particular companies, and investor attitudes toward the companies and the economy. These complex patterns seem undetectable as the magnitude of fluctuation and the timing of different phases of the pattern continually vary. It would be similar to trying to discern the pattern of bright full moons if each full cycle had a different duration and the moon's brightness in different cycles also varied. Given this mathematical challenge, we resort to more readily visible patterns such as previous economic cycles of recession and growth or experiences when the market faced similar interest rates, price-earnings ratios, and corporate profit growth rates. We know these tools are not precise but hope they indicate the underlying pattern.

It has become popular in various kinds of workshops or business meetings to put an issue in front of the group and have the participants write down as many thoughts regarding that issue as possible. They place each thought on a separate post-it note and put those notes on a board. The participants then wander around trying to group the notes into a small number of major categories. This is a process of detecting patterns.

As I mentioned in Chapter 12, the work of John Naisbitt and Patricia Aburdene is a clear example of pattern detection. Their approach is similar to that used by many organizations that accumulate, repackage, and sell information. The accumulation process gathers various types of information from a variety of sources. Pattern detection is the main part of the repackaging process. Naisbitt and Aburdene seek megatrends that will affect everybody. Other organizations may be selling information to different clients. Therefore, they look for patterns relevant to the specific issues faced by the clients. A pattern giving insight to one client may be of only passing interest to another client.

A pattern in information, therefore, is not preordained. We find the pattern for which we are looking. The knowledge base we have been building started with a business field map of a company and its environment. As the map expanded, it grew in complexity. Layer upon layer of detail about forces and players has added to the burden. This base easily becomes overwhelming; there is too much to remember. It is a puzzle with an image that is difficult to detect. This vast knowledge base has numerous patterns. They overlap, each one capturing a different way of organizing the data. We need to discover the patterns.

The business field map displays connections among players but not the significance of the connections; patterns clarify significance. Patterns in the data may not tell us what the future will be but reveal potential strategic opportunities, threats, or constraints that will arise in the future. Patterns describe the existing order within a business' field. Successful strategy cannot ignore them. People are not mechanically locked into patterns, but they do reflect and influence our behavior. Our personal weekday patterns frequently differ from our weekend patterns. Obviously, we choose which pattern to follow. It is similar for the patterns in the business field map; they reflect choice even when we are less aware of it.

Laying the Groundwork (Perceiving)

The five approaches that follow describe different ways to identify patterns.

First approach—Typical key activities or events. This approach is similar to the traffic pattern problem—identify a regularly happening occurrence and then see if that reflects a pattern. Traffic enters and exits freeways; this common activity leads to seeing a pattern. Accidents are relatively typical events. If there is a pattern to accidents—in time, place on the freeway, traffic levels, weather or road conditions—it is possible to take preventive measures or, at least, be prepared to respond to the emergencies. Thinking of your business and the field in which it operates, identify some highly visible or major key events or activities that seem fairly typical, such as customer orders or new product introductions by competitors. These things happen on a frequent basis; therefore, the first pattern to test is whether they happen with clockwork predictability. We may want to know more, however. Are these patterns associated with a noticeable change in an environmental force? Is there a pattern that leads to customer orders or new product introductions? Do customer orders or new product introductions evoke patterns in other players?

Second approach—Seeing commonalties. This approach is similar to the workshop and information analysis examples—look at a large amount of data and determine whether there is a set of patterns that captures most of this data. Obviously, the categories do not spring from the data by themselves. We can use two different methods. One is a relatively intuitive grouping of the data—these things seem similar to other things. The second is to generate different ideas for categories and then test them with the data. Both methods rely upon experience in the business. It is not possible to see groupings or create test categories without confident knowledge about the business. We are seeking association of the data with the category or perhaps signs of causality and results. Let's say one category is labeled *small-scale technology improvements*. As we scan the data with this category in mind, we may find some data that portend the change, some that reflect player response to the change, and some that reveal what the change causes.

Third approach—Testing against known patterns. This approach is similar to the one described in the language and secret code examples—take patterns already known from one experience and apply them to a new one. Perhaps one of the more fruitful approaches is to view your business field through the lens of patterns observed in many business fields. Peter Senge, in his book *The Fifth Discipline*, labels these system archetypes—regularly repeatable cycles of events that help reveal systemic problems a business may face. Adrian J. Slywotzsky, in his book *Value Migration*, identifies seven major industry patterns that reveal how value creation for customers migrates from one type of business to another. It is possible to look at one's business with these patterns and determine whether they are portraying the reality of the business' evolution.

There are many other known patterns. For example, products typically follow a pattern of low sales to early adopters, rapid growth, maturity, and decline. These phases certainly vary in length from one product to another but within any one of them there is also an observable pattern. As individuals age, they seem to follow a pattern. These patterns are not a useful predictor for one person but work in the aggregate. Combining these patterns with population demographics generates foresight about spending and investment patterns. Retail businesses typically have seasonal patterns. Although the pattern may be directly evident in nonretail businesses, we could also take the idea of seasons and see if there are patterns of increased and decreased activities such as production due dates or other deadlines. There are observable patterns that occur as industries evolve in going from low-volume to mass-produced goods to specialized goods. There are patterns of growing customer sophistication as they gain more experience with products. Choose some known patterns and use them for your business field.

Fourth approach—Pattern proxies. This approach is similar to the one described in trying to understand fluctuations in stock market valuations—the true patterns are too difficult to discover, so we use more readily observable indicators of the pattern. Naturally, we want lead indicators that show when the pattern will unfold rather than lag indicators that tell us it has. Trends are often indicators of an underlying pattern; the pattern may be causing the trend. Sometimes it is enough to simply stay with the trend. For example, there is a trend in increased speed of microprocessors. As long as we plan strategy to deal with this trend, we may not need to know the pattern that causes it. The advantage of learning the pattern, perhaps in R&D spending patterns or R&D personnel patterns, is that it becomes possible to know when the trend will shift and act accordingly.

Customer behavior is often the most difficult thing to understand. Millions of dollars are gained and lost as things change in popularity. Years ago, in one of our more unrealistic moments, my wife and I contemplated buying a restaurant at Lake Tahoe. There were a few beautiful buildings housing closed restaurants for sale. The trend for tourism to the region was good, but I wondered why these restaurants, only 1 mile south of the small town, failed while others within and to the east of the town flourished. No one walked; people drove. There was some underlying pattern in dining I could not understand and, therefore, would be at great risk in trying to change.

The best avenue for indicators of change may be interesting pieces of data in your knowledge base that are difficult to understand; you know what the piece of data is, you just do not know what caused it. It may point to a fruitful direction for further information gathering to uncover the pattern. Once you do discover a pattern, you need to decide if you can overcome or change it. After much inquiry of residents, I found that people did not drive in that direction in winter. The road was kept open but there were no major ski areas, hotels, or condominiums in that direction. Given these problems, the pattern would be difficult to change. No one to that point had succeeded; we did not want to try.

Fifth approach—Asking the question. This approach is highly intuitive but it depends upon a strong knowledge base about one's business. We ask and let a pattern arise that gives some sense or direction for figuring out the question. We want to find patterns in the knowledge base relative to important questions. Therefore, the questions should be thought provoking—there are no readily apparent answers. The questions should have major ramifications for the strategic choice—discovering patterns will make a big difference to the strategic possibilities seen. The question could aim at exposing gaps in the knowledge base or current thinking about the knowledge base—trying to find patterns that help resolve significant uncertainties where major assumptions are necessary to proceed to a decision. Finally, the questions need to reflect a willingness to remain in an answering process. The pattern may not be the answer to the question but may help understand the question's issue better.

This is similar to flying over the continent and observing different patterns depending upon what we are trying to learn. If the question is about the origins of cities, we will see the pattern of their location near waterways—the prime transportation system for cities with a longer history. If we want to know about development, we will see patterns of greater construction density near highways and in flatter areas. If we want to know about weather, we will see patterns of wetlands, deserts, and lush or sparse vegetation. All these patterns exist simultaneously but the question draws attention to particular ones.

Clearly, we would not use yes–no or quantitative questions such as *how high will the stock market be?* Or, *will there be sufficient demand for our product?* We would ask questions that could drive us to see patterns in customer behavior such as *how do customer priorities change?* Or, *how do competitors respond to the strategic initiatives of others?* Many of the questions from Chapter 13 regarding understanding future moves by players were questions for which patterns may be useful. The questions should focus thinking and perhaps crystallize a clear path to an answer. You can use questions that directly relate to your product or industry or seem more general such as *which regions of the country will experience growth? Which will experience stagnation?* Experiment with a variety of significant questions for your business and see if outlines of patterns emerge from your business knowledge.

Seeing the Value (Understanding)

There are a few issues to address in gaining understanding about the patterns identified.

- Stability—How long have these patterns been in existence? How much longer are they likely to last?
- Predictability—What do the patterns help predict in the behavior of players in the business field?
- Entrenchment—How difficult is it to influence a change in the patterns?
- Awareness—To what degree are different players aware of the patterns that affect them?

Moving Forward (Reasoning)

Patterns can have several implications for strategy.

- The strategic options to take advantage of existing patterns.
- The possibility of changing or shaping the patterns to the organization's advantage.
- The degree to which existing patterns create an advantage for competitors.
- The possibility of competitors changing or shaping the patterns.
- The way that existing patterns could inhibit the organization's strategic initiatives.
- The implications of this work for further information gathering to build the knowledge base and better understand patterns.

CHAPTER 15

Creating Crystal Balls—
Forming Scenarios

Initial Thoughts

The essence of this process is writing stories about the future as if we were viewing the past.

A scenario is a narrative about the future describing a coherent, plausible, and challenging picture of the confluence of patterns, environmental forces, and players. Scenarios have a value by creating a few distinctive pictures of the future that are likely to have substantively different effects on strategic decisions. We are not predicting the future but creating descriptions of possible futures in order to open thinking and see strategic possibilities. We've done a considerable amount of thinking about the environment; what do scenarios add to that effort?

We have tried to make connections among things, certainly between forces and players, but we have also tended to keep things separate. The future may have many possibilities from our vantage point in the present, but it is only going to become one of those many paths. Please, no Star Trek space-time continuum theories—only one future will happen. We just do not know which one. What we do know is it will be some configuration of forces, players, and patterns. Considering the number of ideas generated in each of these topics, the volume of possible combinations probably would tax the memory of many computers. It is not only beyond our ability to consider them all; it is unnecessary. Many of the combinations would be implausible, others would be inconsistent—the pieces wouldn't fit together, and others would have sufficient similarity that they would add no additional insight. We want combinations that are not only plausible, consistent, and distinctive but also sufficiently interesting to challenge our thinking about strategy. It is analogous to getting dressed in the morning and finding combinations that are aesthetically pleasing and relevant to that day's activities. Ignoring the stylistically untrained, certain colors work together and others do not. Business suits are not worn for physical activities, although the way things are today, the reverse may be true. Scenarios are similar; we are looking for a few combinations that are rich in detail and relevant. It is time for thinking to enter a more convergent path after the intentional divergent directions of the previous thinking processes.

Although one approach for identifying scenarios uses a most likely case, it is not useful to describe a best case and worst case. Once our minds take in those three possibilities, we tend to stay in the midpoint. Best and worst cases are usually modifications, regardless of how dramatic, of the most likely case. They are not distinctive descriptions with very different environmental conditions. This makes the use of scenarios a waste of time. We are going to wind up choosing a strategy that relates to the most likely case, so why bother considering the other two? The kind of thinking we use in best- and worst-case scenarios, however, is useful in testing the viability of a strategy in favorable and unfavorable conditions. It is much better to use that thinking after choosing a single direction for strategy. Chapter 25, "Maneuvering Through Shifting Terrain," addresses this line of thinking. It takes the specific strategic decision and subjects it to variations in the environment to sketch out contingency plans.

In this chapter we are creating scenarios about the future into which we will design strategies—*if this happens, how would we respond?* We are *not* designing alternative strategies and testing their relative worth—*if we did this, what would be the consequences?* The second method has multiple strategies tested against a single environment. We want scenarios to represent multiple environments to give us strategic possibilities. Perhaps one strategy design can effectively meet the challenges of multiple scenarios, but that would be sheer serendipity. Nevertheless, the second method has merit. We gain that value throughout the strategic thinking cycle by continually raising a range of strategic possibilities, testing them against our knowledge base for feasibility, and then choosing among them.

Scenarios describe the kind of futures that may arise, not the kind of future we would like to see. It is possible that subjective views of the future—the degree of optimism or pessimism we possess—influence articulation of scenarios. The following guidance is a simple personal exercise to observe whether personal perspectives of the future influence scenario thinking.

- Considering the future in general, rather than just the future of your business, note your thoughts about what you know, value, have hope for, and fear.
- Identify any assumptions you made for those four categories of thoughts.
- Determine what led to those assumptions, for example, beliefs or information.

- Judge whether there are any facts, ideas, or experiences that would alter those assumptions.
- Determine whether the possible alteration in your assumptions has any influence on your hopes and fears for the future.

As you go through the suggestions in the remainder of the chapter for forming scenarios, notice whether optimism or pessimism is influencing your ideas. We want the scenarios to be relatively objective. Subjectivity is fine for vision and strategic choice, as personal commitment to those decisions and responsibility for their consequences is crucial.

Laying the Groundwork (Perceiving)

First approach—The most likely case. So much work has been done on the environment that there is little doubt that your thinking has begun to converge on a most likely case. You have valid impressions. You have probably formed judgments about the players, forces, and significance of patterns. You may also feel relatively certain or highly confident about these assessments—you believe they will happen. Use your insight to form a scenario. It is certainly plausible and significant to your strategy; you need only synthesize the different ideas to form a single, cohesive view of the future.

The most likely case is an extremely useful scenario. It is probably the one you will use as the central focus for the remainder of the thinking processes. To challenge thinking and discover other considerations to influence the strategic choice, however, a few other scenarios are necessary. In this approach you want to find significant deviations from the most likely case. What could happen that would make it nearly impossible for the most likely scenario to occur? The path to *undermine* the most likely case is to identify the most critical components within it. Which forces, players, or patterns create the crucial link to hold the scenario together? Perhaps there are key assumptions that hold the scenario together. Perhaps a shock wave would change those assumptions or the patterns within the scenario. You are searching for plausible, significant shifts in some part of the environment that will move things in a different direction and lead to distinctive scenarios.

Second approach—What is known and significant. The anchor point in this approach is to start with something well known to the business that forms a major foundation upon which the strategy is likely to be built. Often this foundation is some pattern that seems relatively stable and entrenched. It seems unlikely to change, and a strategy will depend upon its continuation. Form a scenario by looking at environmental changes that would alter the pattern. To form other distinctive scenarios, consider other changes that would alter that pattern or start with a different part of the environment—another pattern, behavior or actions of one or more players, a trend in a force—and look at plausible environmental shifts that would dislodge it.

Third approach—What is unknown and significant. This approach also starts with something important to your business, but this time it revolves around something that is still unresolved. It tends to expand options first, similar to the branching on a tree. You want to choose a key question, decision, or issue that seems to be a focal point for your strategic choice. The intention is to articulate scenarios that offer diverse ways of looking at this focal point so that you can see it from different angles and shape a successful strategy. For example, a key question could be—*how will people view home improvement and remodeling projects?*

We move to our first branching from the focal point by identifying key components of the environment—players, forces, or patterns—that have a direct relationship to the question, decision, or issue and significantly influence the outcome. Influence is the degree to which the component drives the outcome in a positive or negative direction. For the example question there are obvious cost issues for labor and materials, but let's look at several other possibilities—the availability of tradespeople for work, interest rates, new home prices, or the ease of handling do-it-yourself projects.

The second step of branching is to list some discrete possible states for each component. This step is easy to understand through the components in the example. There could be high or low availability of tradespeople; interest rates could be at 4, 6, or 8 percent; new home prices could be declining by 2 percent per month, remaining stable, or increasing by 2 percent per month; and do-it-yourself projects could become easier because of technology or design changes in materials and tools that reduce the level of skills required.

The third step of branching is to list likely causes for each discrete possible state. In the example, several causes affect the availability of labor—general construction activities, ease of obtaining permits for major development projects, wage rates, general state of the economy. Government deficits, potential inflation rates, and economic growth rates influence fluctuations in interest rates. We would follow a similar process for all other states of the different components.

A scenario is nothing more than a plausible combination of causes. We have abstracted from the original focal point to get to larger forces or players in the environment. Given the branching effect of the three steps, however, there are too many combinations to consider. Informed judgment will again lead to a selection of those combinations that challenge thinking to see one's business operating under very different circumstances.

This is a more challenging process than the other two, but its advantage is that it begins with a focal point of something significant the business must resolve. The scenarios create different environments for that focal point, not to resolve it but to fuel thoughts about strategy within those different scenarios. Looking back at the example, suppose the business is a bank trying to design, package, and sell loans for home improvements. The purpose of scenarios is not to determine the feasibility of the entire loan idea but to give conditions that influence the bank's strategy about the loans. The bank can then consider how it designs, packages, and sells the loans under very different circumstances.

Seeing the Value (Understanding)

It is usually valuable to have three of four scenarios. Peter Schwartz (*The Art of the Long View*) suggests naming them to capture their essence and distinctiveness. It is reasonable to include the most likely case in this group as it represents your best judgment on a probable future. You need to decide whether the set of scenarios needs to reflect more and less favorable future possibilities. This understanding phase provides a good test for the distinctiveness of scenarios. They should lead to different mixtures of opportunities, threats, and constraints. The future you and other players face shifts from one scenario to the next—actions, activities, behavior, or direction should be more possible in some scenarios than others. Some scenarios will give some players more favorable conditions or more options. Other scenarios will make things more difficult for some players. To this point we have been thinking about the scenario's favorability or unfavorability to your business; the perspectives of players must also come into consideration. A strategy is not only a response to a scenario about the future but also what different players are likely to face and do within each scenario. Their actions influence your strategic choice.

In this phase, therefore, consider from your perspective and the perspective of different key players how the scenarios differ in closing or opening some opportunities, posing new threats, defusing old threats, reinforcing or diminishing constraints to business initiatives. Consider likely responses by different players to the opportunities, threats, and constraints they face in different scenarios.

Moving Forward (Reasoning)

Identify your own strategic options in each scenario. Consider your best path in these scenarios given the opportunities, threats, and constraints your business will face and your assessment of the likely responses of different players to the conditions they face. It is also possible that this work will expose new key questions, decisions, or issues for the third approach to perceiving scenarios. If so, decide whether another pass at creating scenarios would be beneficial to thinking about strategy.

CHAPTER 16

Just When You Thought
It Was Safe—
Navigating Shock Waves

Initial Thoughts

The essence of this process is perceiving the unexpected.

There is a tendency in foreseeing the future to simply project trends in environmental forces as we detect patterns and form scenarios. Yet the major opportunities and threats caused by these forces often come from significant changes not easily predicted by simply looking at the past. These changes are often quite difficult to anticipate as they represent such a radical departure from present conditions. For example, many major world events—the collapse of communism in Eastern Europe, the prospects for peace in the Middle East, the rapidly improving political and economic stability throughout Latin America—were difficult to foresee and certainly not extensions of the past or present. Major discontinuities are so elusive because they challenge our experience of the world and the paradigms we hold.

Major technological changes are occurring in areas such as biotechnology, communications, and computerization. Major technological advances have the prospect for significant changes in all of society, in the basic industrial fabric or infrastructure, and in seemingly unrelated industries. The automobile industry did not just change the market for the proverbial buggy-whip manufacturers but altered housing patterns, tourism, industry location, and probably a multitude of other products and services that do not directly think of themselves as being in the transportation industry.

This process contains a challenging paradox of strategic thinking—predict the unpredictable. Karl Albrecht, in *The Northbound Train*, defines a shock wave as, "An irreversible trend or movement powerful enough to restructure the basic realities of doing business." When the shock wave hits there is no turning back; things cannot return to their former state and businesses will have trouble pursuing the paths they had previously chosen. A shock wave is a major unexpected event, a radical departure from the present. Although it is necessary to allow some creative speculating about the future, the shock wave needs to be plausible.

Shock waves dislodge the status quo; contemplation of them should certainly shake our thinking. We have been following a seemingly logical train of thought—creating a field map of the business environment, analyzing the forces and players in that environment, seeking some foresight about the future often using trends from the present, detecting patterns amidst the mass of information and knowledge to simplify it and find some connections among things, and forming scenarios from that knowledge base to create a few distinct, coherent images of the future.

We thought we were closing in on strategy. Now shock waves have arrived to throw us back and move us out of the comfort of our previous thought. Shock waves are a jolt to logic that tear up entrenched patterns, rock them from their foundations of stability, and reduce any sense of predictability from them. Shock waves cause us to return to our scenarios and realize that even the most likely case could include a shock wave looming on the horizon.

Shock waves are massive environmental changes. Maybe we restricted our imaginations when we tried to get alternative scenarios. Shock waves will alter that. What kind of scenarios would you now create if you included different shock waves? Just remember as you move from the complacency of your current thought patterns that shock waves are not like brainstorming. We are not trying to encourage a large number of ideas, no matter how wild or unfeasible. Shock waves are real events that dramatically alter the landscape, making business as usual unfeasible. Even if they have a low likelihood of occurring, you can articulate good reasons for them happening.

Frequently, the phrase *shock wave* evokes images of catastrophe and we consider the horrible things that can happen. Why do our minds get drawn to the negative side more rapidly? This is not disaster planning. A massive weather problem that greatly disrupts business is a significant issue needing attention. It is not a shock wave; it has not altered the course of events. Recovery and a return to normality are the issues, not developing a new strategic direction. A shock wave is simply a significant discontinuity from the present. It is a serious threat to those trying to keep themselves in the same place, but it holds opportunity for those with the acuity to ride it. This is the power of a vibrant economy. Every creative act builds as well as destroys—something new replaces something old. Every major event brings potential as well as hazard. The economist Joseph Schumpeter appropriately labeled this phenomenon *creative destruction*. The possibility that major events could alter strategic plans is an important subject deserving serious attention.

. . . you better start swimmin'
Or you'll sink like a stone.
For the times they are a-changin'.

BOB DYLAN

Laying the Groundwork (Perceiving)

If it is a shock wave, we cannot know what will happen. We are only trying to think about what could happen. This is not a process of prediction, although it is possible to identify an impending shock wave. The major intent, however, is to become mentally prepared to respond to large changes that completely alter the context for one's business. To identify possible shock waves, or as it is more appropriately called, *perceive the imperceivable*, I want to suggest a few alternative ways of thinking about the whole environment. Each approach opens one's mind to seeing possible shock waves. Different approaches could easily lead to the same shock waves. Use them in any order or select the ones that seem most relevant to your business. Furthermore, remember that this process is useful only if it creates foresight about the future that is distinctive from the previous thinking processes for the environment. The search is to identify how shock waves dramatically alter the conditions surrounding the business, closing or opening some opportunities, posing new threats, defusing old threats, reinforcing or diminishing constraints to the business' initiatives.

In Chapter 11 we created a map representing the network of relationships to define the field in which a business operates. That map is a snapshot of the present. As we put the map in motion, trying to get a sense of the dynamic nature of the field, we are thinking about the various transactions that take place among players on the field. In Chapter 12 on the thinking process about the economic, political, technological, and social forces in the business environment we looked at known changes, predicted changes, or changes that had important but contained impacts. We traced these changes through the map's existing transactions to determine impacts on a business. In this thinking process we are trying to adapt to possible massive shifts in the future.

Shock waves are major changes in which the transactions themselves change and some players may change. It is a process of speculation rather than prediction. It is more of a *what if* approach rather than an *I believe the following could happen* approach. In Chapter 12 the image to understand the influence of environmental forces was a pebble dropped in a pond; after some iterations, the business would feel the effects. This is more of a tidal wave that overthrows expectations and thrusts us into new terrain. The effects may even increase in magnitude as a shock wave has multiple effects throughout the map. For example, Hong Kong reverting to Chinese control is a significant change but we knew it would happen and could plan for it. China adopting the Hong Kong approach to business throughout the rest of the country would be a shock wave. A vaccine to prevent AIDS is a shock wave. The gas price increase in the 1970s was a shock wave. The high interest rates from the late 1970s to the early 1980s was a shock wave.

First approach—Breaking the lines of predictions. The last few examples indicate a simple but fertile ground for exploring shock waves. A shock wave is a discontinuity. Most work on environment forces relies on determining what is likely to happen. Take each force identified and look at radical departures from what you considered likely to happen. It is a different question to ask where the economy is heading than what possible economic conditions could occur. Therefore, a scan of the world—economically, technologically, socially, and politically—can open sources of shock waves. We are considering *what the world can look like* rather than *what it is likely to look like* over the next few years.

For example, on a geopolitical scale it is possible to think of several major changes. What if terrorism increases? What if trouble spots around the world become more peaceful? What if there is a dramatic opening in free trade? These questions lead us to look at different types of changes in the transactions and players. How could that shock wave create a need for new transactions, such as increasing demand for new products or services? How could that shock wave make existing transactions irrelevant, such as reducing or eliminating demand for some products and services? How could that shock wave cause players to become more (or less) important in some transactions, such as accelerating or diminishing the distinctive value their products provide to customers? How could that shock wave cause players to alter the roles they assume, such as customers now becoming competitors?

Second approach—Vulnerability. Vulnerability to shock waves can occur through the forces that are most critical to a business but for which there is the least knowledge or the greatest uncertainty. Whereas the first approach had a wide scan view of the environment, this approach starts with the business. It is dependent for its success on the state of some environmental force but lacks knowledge about that force or has great uncertainty about it. Choose forces you feel most critical to your business and about which you know the least or have the greatest uncertainty. These are forces for which future predictions were extremely tenuous. Tenuous means that the force can move in widely divergent directions and there is no effective way to predict the direction it will take. For example, at the time of this writing, as the bull stock market roars on after a 6-year run, many people predict a reversal, but money keeps pouring in, even given the temporary reversal of February and March 1997. The experts are divided; it is possible to receive every conceivable piece of advice. What are the effects of a dramatic and longer run decline? What are the effects of several more years of increase?

Third approach—Taking things for granted. The success of any business frequently depends upon things taken for granted—the telecommunications and transportation infrastructure, the educational system, the dominance of the U.S. dollar in international commerce. We do not pay attention to these things because they have always been there, in our experience, and we implicitly assume they will continue. Therefore, it is prudent to identify some of these *out-of-view* dependencies and think about significant changes that would create a shock wave for your business. Use patterns that you consider stable or well-entrenched to imagine realistic shock waves that would alter or end the patterns.

Fourth approach—If only. Perhaps one of the easier ways to identify shock waves is to imagine some things we would love to see happen. We can do this from the perspective of the business, from the perspective of being a citizen of the world, or simply from our day-to-day experiences of the problems and issues we face. *If only* we faced a less litigious society. . . . *If only* Democrats and Republicans operated government as if solving problems and building public confidence mattered. . . . *If only* ethnic and religious differences were a source of growth rather than virulent antagonisms. . . . *If only* there was reduced rush hour traffic. . . .

Fifth approach—Uh-oh. The flip side of what we would love to see happen is what we would fear to see happen. This approach returns us to our earlier bias about shock waves—they have catastrophic effects. These are the shock waves that seriously damage the entire business climate or completely erode demand for your product. Of course, one business' *if only* can be another business' *uh-oh*. Consider technological breakthroughs that make things readily affordable to large numbers of people, such as decentralized solar power generation, widespread wireless communication, or electric cars that go a month between battery charges.

Sixth approach—Back to the drawing board. If we look at the whole flow of the strategic thinking cycle we have more processes to cover before a strategic decision. It would be unnatural, useless, and wrong to go through these processes in a purely sequential order without having the mind leap to some strategic possibilities. These thinking processes that view the business' environment from various perspectives and to varying degrees of depth push thinking outward, expanding the net of knowledge, so that a wider range of strategic possibilities come into view. If a good idea shows up, why not pursue it? There is no sense in staying in this more divergent thought mode if there is an idea worth testing. In fact, I think it is a good discipline in these earlier stages of the cycle to simply say, *if I had to choose a strategy right now, based on what I know to this point, what would I do?* In this approach we can look at this tentative choice and try to identify some of the reasons for it. These reasons will contain some relationship to environmental forces. Shock waves, therefore, are *unexpected* changes to these forces that would make the tentative decision completely inaccurate.

It is possible these various approaches uncovered shock waves that portend big changes but seem rather unlikely. They may signal other crucial areas of vulnerability or possibility for your business. For example, suppose you looked at the decline of the U.S. dollar dominance. Although history tells us that all great civilizations fade from power, we may believe that unlikely in the more immediate future for the U.S. economy. Following that as a shock wave, however, may reveal the importance of international commerce to your business. It would then be worthwhile to pursue possible shock waves in that arena.

Seeing the Value (Understanding)

The perceiving part of this thinking process could generate a large number of shock waves. In this part we want to focus attention on those that are most important. We do this by considering the relative likelihood of those shock waves occurring and the extent of their effects on the business. How do we assess relative likelihood? It is purely a subjective judgment. If it is a shock wave, it is not a repeated event with a long history from which we could calculate probabilities. We can only look at the range of shock waves identified and try to rank them by our best guess on likelihood, not what we desire to happen or not happen. We also want this ranking to be independent of the assessment of the impact on the business.

If it is relatively natural to think about possible strategies, it is certainly reasonable to move to this intermediate step first. Each approach identified a variety of shock waves. It would be difficult to identify them without considering the significance to your own business. As the shock wave roars through the business field map it changes players and the transactions among them. We would want to know what those changes mean for the business. These impacts can be summarized, as we did earlier in this chapter, in how the cumulative effects of the shock wave close or open some opportunities, pose new threats, defuse old threats, and reinforce or diminish constraints to the business' initiatives. Most shock waves will have benefits and costs. You cannot control a shock wave; you look to find a way to survive or thrive in its presence.

Moving Forward (Reasoning)

In this part of the process we would tend to focus thinking on those shock waves that had the largest impact and the highest likelihood. There are several conclusions reachable at this point for the more significant shock waves.

- Tentative ideas about strategic direction if the shock wave occurs.
- Possible methods to track information that would help anticipate the arrival of the shock wave.
- Triggers that would serve as warning signals to detect the shock wave in its early stages.
- The resources the company is willing to devote to maintain a state of preparedness for the potential arrival of a shock wave.

Intermission

CHAPTER 17

A Minor Exploratory Interlude—Eclectic Analogies

It is time for a break, of sorts. We have come partway around the strategic cycle, investing much thought in understanding the environment surrounding the business and alternative futures for that environment. Throughout those thinking processes, ideas for strategies emerge. We are about to follow that line of thought into greater depth by moving into the focusing phases of identifying strategic possibilities, matching the possibilities with capabilities, choosing one possibility for a strategy, and making the strategy work.

Although previous processes expanded thinking, they all concentrated on business-related content. This chapter's process may appear as a diversion from the task at hand. It opens thinking to very different possibilities. Sometimes we become so embedded in a given industry or market or so enamored of our products that we lose the ability to see very different alternatives. Paradigms and implicit assumptions about an industry, market, or product often limit thinking. We need to break some of these thought patterns by thinking about something completely different. Eclectic analogies cause us to leap completely away from the prevailing paradigms, by using knowledge of diverse fields such as arts or science, to gain different insights into strategy. We can draw parallels from these fields to business.

You can get a sense of eclectic analogies by thinking about different interests you have or things that you have read and ask yourself, *what have I learned from that experience that has value to me beyond that experience?* For example, a person with strong interest in river rafting could see it as a metaphor for an organization and the way teams must work to navigate a challenging environment. With this knowledge the manager could have a valuable impact on the success of teams. It is not surprising that rafting is a common team-building exercise. A person with interests in music may notice that most great music seems to successfully evoke an emotion and might wonder if that approach could guide the design of the way a customer experiences a company and its product or services.

With substantive knowledge of biological systems (e.g., the human body, gardening, or forestry) you would have interesting insights into organizations. You simply say to yourself, what if an organization is similar to a human body (garden or forest)? Knowing what causes health and disease in biology, you could draw ideas about what might create health and stagnation in an organization. You could look at how biological systems grow, maintain a constant state, or deal with changing environmental conditions. From these you could think about ways the organization could grow, maintain some stability, and be flexible to meet unexpected changes. Similar analogies could be drawn from gardening or forestry.

This approach has a rich background in many business books. David Whyte has explored the power of poetry in *The Heart Aroused: Poetry and the Preservation of the Soul in Corporate America*. Margaret Wheatley has tapped into recent explorations in physics in *Leadership and the New Science: Learning about Organizations from an Orderly Universe*. Carol Pearson and Sharon Seivert have unveiled insights into mythological archetypes in *Magic at Work: A Guide to Releasing Your Highest Creative Powers*. There have been numerous adaptations of Lao Tzu's ancient classic, the *Tao Te Ching* (John Heider, *The Tao of Leadership*; Bob Messing, *The Tao of Management*, Cresencio Torres, *The Tao of Teams*).

The common theme of all these books is to enter a realm of knowledge that at first seems completely unrelated to business. The authors transfer ideas from that realm to the general business arena to derive insights into ways of managing or leading people and the whole organization. For strategy there have been very obvious translations from ancient literature—Sun Tzu's *Art of War* and Miyamoto Musashi's *A Book of Five Rings*. All strategy concentrates on a few simple issues: understanding the world around us, seeing the possibilities that await us in the future, and finding a way to navigate ourselves into that uncertain future by exploiting the chosen opportunities and meeting any threats. These are questions that have faced humanity for centuries, whether the community is trying to survive or progress.

In an earlier chapter I said that good strategic thinkers were well informed. Here I am saying that good strategic thinkers are also well rounded. One's highest expertise usually falls in one's career, but that does not preclude other interests not directly related to career. In this process we are synthesizing the insights contained within those other interests with the strategic needs of the organization. Eclectic analogies should be enjoyable; they are most useful if they create ways of looking at a business that the other thinking processes miss.

Choose areas of personal interest and knowledge you have outside the business world in fields such as art, culture, literature, science, sports, or hobbies. Identify the wisdom in that field through a variety of areas. The first one is the field's essential activities. For example, in carpentry essential activities may include the design process, selection of woods, and the producing process. The second is the field's views of the world, systems, or people. In carpentry these views may include the relation of the craft to other crafts and the training process from apprentice to master. The third one is the field's basic assumptions, beliefs, and paradigms. In carpentry these perspectives may include some balance among efficiency, functionality, uniqueness, and aesthetics. The fourth one is the field's appeal or attraction to participants. In carpentry this appeal may include the use of one's hands, feel of the wood, artisanship, or enjoyment in the quality of the tools of the trade.

Having described a field using these four areas, we need to understand the key insights. We get these by seeing the description in more generalizable terms. For example, what does the carpentry design process reveal about design in general? What are the important things considered in selecting woods that could help other selection processes such as choice of suppliers or personnel hiring procedures? What can we learn from carpentry's focus on balancing among efficiency, functionality, uniqueness, and aesthetics? To complete the process, apply these generalized insights to specific, significant aspects of your environment knowledge base, business, or current thoughts about strategy.

PART 4

Talking the Walk—
Deciding What to Do

Identifying Strategic Levers for Competitive Advantage

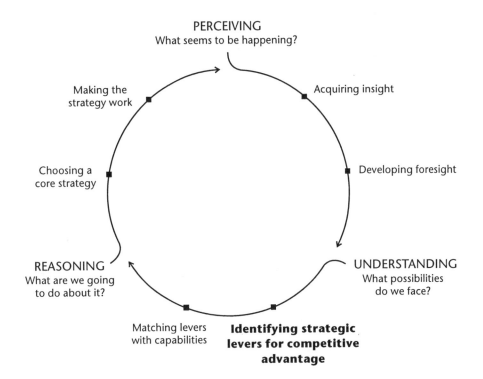

PERCEIVING
What seems to be happening?

Making the
strategy work

Acquiring insight

Choosing a
core strategy

Developing foresight

REASONING
What are we going
to do about it?

UNDERSTANDING
What possibilities
do we face?

Matching levers
with capabilities

**Identifying strategic
levers for competitive
advantage**

CHAPTER 18

Making a Difference— Delivering Value

Initial Thoughts

The essence of this process is identifying possibilities for competitive advantage in delivering value that best satisfies customer priorities.

A Brief Review

Welcome back from the interlude. As we are now moving into the thought processes that lead toward a strategy, it will be useful to have a quick review of the ground already covered. We have looked at several processes that were only in the perceiving phase of the strategic thinking cycle. This has been a path of building a knowledge base from which strategy emerges. It is a widening net, getting broader and more in-depth knowledge about current conditions in the business and moving toward alternative ways of viewing possible futures. It is natural when thinking about the environment of a business to have these more descriptive thoughts followed by some ideas of possibilities and what the business could do to succeed. Recognizing this natural flow of thought, the thinking process covered in each chapter moved toward tentative conclusions. It is frustrating to halt the flow of thoughts that identify some ideas for strategy. The important thing is to avoid becoming too attached to one strategy before thinking moves through a variety of possibilities.

We began with a business field map—a simple visual display of the relationships among players. We extended this map past the restricted view of a single industry to answer the question, *what business are we really in?* We placed this field map in the *whirling maze* of forces—economic, technological, social, and political. These affect the players and their relationships. We also looked at how these forces may be trending into the future. We then returned to the players to build up more detailed knowledge about each one.

As this knowledge base broadens and deepens, it becomes apparent that one must constantly exercise judgment about what seems more central and more peripheral to one's business. As we drop things from consideration we are making a decision to take the risk of not following that information any further. We also notice that no matter how much information we have obtained about the players and the forces, there is always something more we would like to know. Often, however, we cannot find the appropriate data or information, so we have a continuing need to make assumptions. This should not surprise us. Strategy is about the future. We are uncertain about how things will unfold in the future but we need to make decisions. Assumptions and uncertainty are tied together. We try to pursue more information if we feel that the assumptions are very tenuous— they reflect a high degree of uncertainty about the future.

We moved to detecting patterns—a method of trying to simplify the complexity created through this expanding field map and depth of information. Patterns that exist in the way the industry or different players operate and respond to changes help create a picture of what we face in the future. We generated understanding of patterns by looking at things such as their stability, predictability about the future, and degree of entrenchment. That allowed us to think about the implications of choosing strategies that change patterns, flow with the patterns, or swim upstream against them. We sought a more convergent view of the future by creating a few distinctive scenarios—coherent, plausible, and challenging narratives of alternative mixtures of patterns, environment forces and players. To give us different perspectives on the future we looked at navigating *shock waves*—major shifts in the environment that can completely alter the business field map. We may think of shock waves as unexpected, but it is poor strategic judgment to wait until things happen and then begin to react. We identified a range of shock waves to see how they would alter the future and how we could sense their arrival.

Strategic Levers

These next three chapters are the beginning of the understanding phase of the major strategic thinking cycle—*what possibilities do we face?* They focus on three strategic levers for competitive advantage: delivering value, shifting paradigms, and selecting critical success factors. They build on the knowledge base from the prior work. Therefore, the issues covered in the initial phase of each of these three thinking processes provide slightly different ways of looking at information already present. I think they capture in simple form the main areas in which a company can get an edge on its competitors. They are powerful mechanisms to leverage growth—gaining market share, increasing sales volume, seeking new markets, and introducing new products. Growth is the only realistic direction for strategy. Receding is not an appealing option. Staying the same and holding on to the status quo is nearly impossible in a changing world that includes other companies seeking growth. If things are relatively stable and it is possible to keep the same position, there is no need for strategy. The only source of improvement in a relatively static world is operational planning that focuses on efficiency and cost control. On the other hand, strategic leverage derives from the small investment in organized thinking that leads to new insights about the business.

Priorities and Values

If you build a better mousetrap, the world will beat a path to your door. If you believe that, you could become very lonely waiting. The fallacy of the first statement frequently serves as the rationale for effective marketing. Customers are relatively passive; they need promotion and advertising to draw them to the product. Marketing is useful, but it is not the best route to understanding the reason for the statement's fallacy. What does *better* mean? Is it infallible? Is it easy to use? Is it safe around pets and small children? Does it kill the mice or trap them for later release? Is it some combination of these considerations? Does *better* mean different things to different customers? Why trap mice anyway? Can we stop them from showing up? Can we get a Pied Piper to attract them and bring them somewhere else?

From the customer perspective there is no focus on mousetraps; the issue is unwanted pests. A mousetrap manufacturer may have great R&D leading to sophisticated mousetraps and good marketing skills to draw customers. The manufacturer begins to think that the product is a customer priority. That is a dangerous belief. A customer priority may be quite simple—no mice. Striving to deliver value that satisfies that priority is the nature of the competitive challenge; building better mousetraps is only one alternative.

W. L. Gore does not make clothing; they sell *Gore-Tex*. Dupont does not make carpets; they sell *Stainmaster*. Intel does not make computers; they sell *Pentium* chips. Consumers, while buying clothing, carpets, and computers, are seeking the value provided by these manufacturers. The clothing manufacturer's label may have less influence on the sale than the Gore-Tex label. Most people do not know the names of carpet manufacturers. It is possible that the names of computer manufacturers will diminish in importance as consumers have more experience with the product. Gore, Dupont, and Intel have all grasped an important consumer priority and positioned themselves to be a major deliverer of the desired value. To the extent that they have successfully tuned in to customer priorities, they could easily receive more net profit from each consumer product sale than the manufacturers of the clothing, carpets, and computers.

The situation is the same for any consumer, end user, or customer; priorities drive purchase decisions. The priorities have one major source—*what is the purchaser trying to create?* We usually talk about needs, wants, or ability to pay. Economists focus on maximizing utility. These different concepts may help, but the truth is simple—people will pay for what they value. When commercial customers buy a product or service they are trying to produce and deliver something for their customers, so the source of their priorities is clear. Specific priorities derive from things that make their work easier, more profitable, or more distinctive relative to their competitors in satisfying their customer's priorities. Consumers do not think in terms of customers; nevertheless, they are always trying to create something with the products or services they buy. You can test this thought simply. When you buy a car, what are your priorities? When you go out to a restaurant, what are your priorities? Look at any consumer purchase decision you make; your priorities depend upon how you intend to use the product or service.

Priorities are expressions of what the customer values. Often we dismiss their priorities as being perceived rather than real—they think they need something rather than really needing it. In a relatively affluent society, there are very few things customers really need. Nearly everything purchased represents choice rather than compulsion. Once we enter the realm of choice we are also in the realm of perceived needs. It is irrelevant if we regard some needs as important and others as less important. It is more important to understand which priorities are relatively stable and which are more subject to change. Fads clearly reflect the changing nature of priorities. When immersed in the fad, however, the value for the product or service seems as real as most other needs. It will always be beneficial to see priorities mostly originating in the use of a product or service. Quality issues are integrally related to those priorities. Quality is nothing more than a product attribute that has merit in the eyes of the customer. It is not some separate characteristic that stands on it own unconnected to customer use of the product.

The Competitive Realm

Sony's Betamax may have had superior picture quality. Apple has continued to design a more user-friendly operating system. These features met an important consumer priority, but it was not enough. Consumers had a different priority that was more commanding—flexibility in use. By Sony and Apple controlling technology through limited licensing, consumers faced limited options. Monopolies protected through patents are completely vulnerable when customers have alternatives and do not want to feel compelled to depend upon a single manufacturer.

Power and profits in any business will invariably flow to the companies best positioned to deliver the value that satisfies customer priorities. It is not surprising that Microsoft seems more significant than IBM. It is the software people want; the hardware gives them access to it. The power can easily shift again—what people really want is the capability that software gives them. The proliferation of personal computers has already led to redundancy in computer storage and software programs. The next evolution of the industry can easily be technology that gives people easy, secure access to some central depository of memory and programs. A new form of time-sharing can easily arise in the future. Creating these alternatives may eliminate a main reason that drives so many people to spend sizable amounts of money to have their own computers and their own software.

The only thing we know for certain is that nothing stays the same. Any customer wants priorities satisfied and even those priorities change over time. When the priorities shift to price, however, watch out. The product is bordering on becoming a commodity. The customers see insufficient difference in the value delivered by competing companies. Companies facing these conditions often attempt to differentiate themselves from competitors. More often than not, these efforts add cost with little distinctive value for which the customer is willing to pay. Airlines have gone through many phases of this battle—piano bars in the top level of 747s, large amounts of food, and frequent flier programs. These programs may gain loyalty with some individual customers but all airlines have them. The impact is probably increased operating cost with the distribution of fliers among airlines remaining relatively unchanged. These bonuses may be attractive, but they do not address customer priorities. It is all tenuous, however. It is very easy to slip into a commodity. The recurrent price wars attest to that fact. The main thing that has kept airlines afloat—or in the air—is price differentiation. They charge vastly different prices to a range of customers for the same flight, seat, and meal—a practice that would be impossible, if not illegal, for most other companies.

The airline price differentiation does pick up differences in customer priorities. They capture these priorities in their rules—Saturday night stays, advance purchase, and nonrefundable or changeable tickets. Different customers will pay different amounts for essentially the same product or service because they vary in their priorities. Most companies do not have the ability to extract the extra revenue from the customers who would be willing to pay more than the going market price. Test this wedge between delivered value and price for some products you buy. Would you be willing to pay more for some of them? What percentage price increase would cause you not to buy the product? This reveals one of the reasons for the financial success of Gore, Dupont, and Intel. By driving up the demand for their customers' products, they are able to get their prices closer to the value they deliver. Therefore, as we explore opportunities for delivering value, a key idea is to move into that position where your customers experience your company as critical to delivering the value they need to satisfy their priorities. It may mean higher prices and profits, more customer loyalty, or increased volume. Alternatives need to be less satisfactory to them.

Through the phases of the thinking process the entire discussion of values and priorities filters into strategic possibilities for your organization. The intent is to uncover alternatives for leveraging existing and changing priorities and value delivery to your advantage. You want the value you deliver to be a significant part of the field. You want to occupy a difficult-to-assail position in value delivery. This is a main part of the competitive battleground; as the value delivered shrinks, a company's position becomes increasingly weaker. One thing any company looks for is ways to shift value delivery to their domain. Things will not remain static. You can trace the dynamic nature of any business through the way value delivery shifts from one company to another—from hardware to software in the computer industry, from carpet or clothing manufacturers to Dupont or Gore, and so on. Value delivery shifts when some companies are better positioned than others to satisfy existing, changing, or emerging priorities. They may even be able to create new priorities customers had not previously considered. Economists tell us that businesses maximize profits. Profit levels are an important goal, but they are a result of where the real attention should be—maximizing the delivery of value.

Laying the Groundwork (Perceiving)

The place to start this thinking process is with the players on the business field map. You want to know one simple thing for the individual players—*what are they trying to create and, therefore, what are their priorities*? Most of the discussion in this chapter has centered on customers but it is also valuable to have this insight for other players—strategic partners, suppliers, distributors, and providers of complementary products and services. Finding ways to help other players satisfy their priorities can give a business a more secure position. The answer to this question for the players may be right at hand from previous thinking processes that built a knowledge base to understand the players. The information is available; now it is necessary to identify what is of utmost importance to each player.

Many of the players are other businesses—their priorities stem from the value they try to deliver to their customers. Therefore, the answer to the question above is not easily found by looking at each player in isolation. Each player is part of a chain leading from one customer to the next, finally reaching some end user or final consumer. Connections among these chains form the network of player relationships on the business field map. When the customer to end user chains have many links, it may be possible to understand different player priorities by looking only at them, their immediate customers, and a couple of additional links. Frequently, there are fewer links and the broader perspective on each player is easier to grasp.

We start with end users or consumers; they do not have customers to whom they are trying to deliver value. Their priorities stem from their own use of the product or service. Gore, Dupont, and Intel advertise to consumers to create a demand for the products from retail stores and manufacturers. Pharmaceutical companies advertise to consumers to create a demand for the drugs from physicians. Advertising is a communication mechanism that works only if it accurately targets a consumer priority. Let's look at one example. Gore works toward the consumer priority for outdoor active wear that is waterproof and breathable. Retailers will carry merchandise with Gore-Tex material but they also need to meet other customer priorities for variety of merchandise, style, color, and available stock. Retailers may have other priorities that enable them to meet the customer priorities such as quick order time and credit terms. Clothing manufacturers will respond to these priorities with an additional priority of remaining competitive in the design and variety of clothing lines. It becomes quite clear that it is in Gore's interest to aid manufacturer design of clothing, innovate new uses, and uphold the guarantee for the Gore-Tex material's effectiveness. Gore-Tex clothing is only a piece of the business of the manufacturers and retailers; they sell a wider range of merchandise. Effectively delivering value to them requires an understanding of their entire business.

There are similar analyses for other players. Your suppliers should be operating to satisfy your priorities; after all, you are the customer. That does not mean they do that successfully. Understanding their business—their suppliers, competitors, other customers, and so forth—may allow you to see how they could improve their ability to deliver value. Strategic partners and suppliers of complementary products are also recipients and deliverers of value. They have their priorities connected to their view of customers or chains of customers. Their relationship or connection to your business and to their suppliers influences how they deliver value.

Seeing the Value (Understanding)

By looking at the business field map we get an idea of the current state of priorities. We can also assess whether different players are adequately delivering value to satisfy priorities of their customers. Regardless of that detail, the map is still a static picture. The real challenges begin as things move into the future—that is the dynamic nature of the map. We have created many ideas about the future of the environment; now it is time to incorporate that understanding into this work on delivering value. The key question is simple—*how do changes in the environment influence priorities and delivering value to satisfy those priorities?*

Consider the following issues. *As interest rates fluctuate, do priorities change? As people age, do their priorities change? As new technology is introduced, do priorities change? As the economy grows, do priorities change? As companies merge and restructure, do priorities change?* The answer to all questions is *yes*. Some priorities may be relatively stable regardless of changes in the environment but many depend upon a set of circumstances; change the circumstances and the priorities will follow.

The first view into the future is the *most likely case* scenario. That is the one you believe will occur. Therefore, as that future comes into being, how will it affect the priorities of different players? Does it affect the abilities of different players to deliver value?

Take the alternative scenarios next. Their distinctiveness exists as an alternative future that may have different shifts in priorities and value delivery. What if the priorities remain relatively similar? Does that mean the scenario is useless? It is, if nothing else changes to give you a different angle on strategy. This may be a good check on the scenarios. It may be necessary to revisit them and create ones that do result in changing priorities.

Scenarios should capture most of the trends in environmental forces. If you have thought about other changes in environmental forces that have not become part of a scenario, use these to see if they influence changes in priorities and value delivery.

Shift to the detected patterns and determine whether any of them reveal how priorities change or how the delivery of value shifts in the industry. Follow this last line of thought to see new players emerging who can deliver value to satisfy existing, changing, or emerging priorities through different products, services, or methods that your industry would consider *nontraditional*.

Shock waves, as traumatic or exciting as they may be, often do not appear in scenarios. Although we tried to identify several, we think of them as unexpected. By upsetting patterns, shock waves affect the *rules of the game*; priorities are bound to shift. Revisit shock waves you identified and note the influence on priorities and value delivery.

Remember that throughout this phase you are trying to retain the spirit of the business field map—understanding the future through the perspectives of different players.

Moving Forward (Reasoning)

The understanding phase created a broad scope of future views. You now want to delineate strategic possibilities you face to respond to the range of opportunities, threats, and constraints these future views hold for the delivery of value.

An opportunity is an opening in the future to expand your delivery of value or make it more distinctive and attain a more secure position. Strategic possibilities fall into several areas for positioning your company, products or services to deliver value:

- Meeting current customer priorities.
- Identifying current priorities that are not being completely satisfied.
- Aiding suppliers, distributors, strategic partners, or providers of complementary products to improve their delivery of value.
- Targeting priorities of consumers or other customers farther down the chain from you to create a demand on your direct customers.
- Positioning to meet the evolution of the industry as priorities shift in response to changes in anything external to your business—environmental forces or shock waves.
- Emphasizing different value delivery as an industry follows its normal pattern of progress or decline.
- Altering the value chains or networks on the map by expanding to deliver value currently being offered by other players.
- Moving into new lines of business where you can change the prevailing rules for delivering value.

- Influencing a change of priorities to more closely match the value you deliver.
- Inducing new priorities where you have a value delivery edge.
- Identifying ways to respond to value delivery moves by other players that also may be changing things to your advantage.
- Following the lead of competitors or other players who initiate successful moves to deliver value or change priorities.

A threat is an action by a player or a change in a force that can diminish your delivery of value. It occurs when there is a change or an evolution of the industry away from your line of business. It happens when competitors aggressively duplicate your successful efforts. It takes place when competitors or other players initiate moves similar to those in the preceding list that will work to your disadvantage. Initial thoughts may naturally move to methods to keep your position form eroding. We know, however, that maintaining the status quo is impossible; something must change. There is no purely defensive action. Sustaining a viable position requires definite action on one or more of the items on the list. Think ahead of competitors and other players by looking at the value delivery moves from their perspectives—what are they positioned to do? Anticipation is necessary. The approach here is similar to the intent for exploring thinking as a competitive advantage—using a variety of perspectives to convert knowledge about the present into glimpses of the future and a range of possible actions.

A constraint is anything in the environment that severely restrains your ability to pursue your initiatives to deliver value. They are not threats; threats can shrink your business or your options. Constraints make it difficult for you to expand and hold you to a current position. Look at the strategic possibilities you considered from the list and identify environmental factors—players, forces, shock waves, or patterns—that block your ideas. Consider how you could alter these strategic possibilities to overcome the hurdles.

CHAPTER 19

Moving Against the Grain— Shifting Paradigms

Initial Thoughts

The essence of this process is leveraging paradigms to one's competitive advantage.

We have returned to paradigms—it is jargon that is hard to avoid. Paradigms—sets of beliefs or assumptions—give us a view of the world, a way of making sense of our surroundings. We cannot live without them. We need a frame of reference. Every culture is a paradigm—a way of thinking about people, relationships among them, and the world in which they live. Paradigms lead to cultural patterns we call rituals, taboos, and so forth. No culture is the truth; no culture is false. They are what they are. Diversity training and increased ability to operate globally depend on developing the ability to move among cultures. That ability requires one to shift among paradigms—without judging what is right or wrong—to see things through a different perspective. Moving through a variety of strategic thinking processes is a mechanism to allow similar flexibility. If we are good strategic thinkers, we may feel more comfortable with our own paradigms, but we can readily shift our minds to other ones.

We do not want to become trapped in paradigms, seeing the world through only one filter, and miss opportunities. Paradigms can limit thinking when they fall below the surface of our awareness. We then act is if we have the truth. It may seem like an act of hubris, but it is nothing more than inattention to the underlying structure of our thoughts. We become so accustomed to the paradigms of our own culture, upbringing, experience, or industry that we ignore the possibility of other, equally valid, views of reality. We forget that the same paradigm that aids our understanding also creates subconscious barriers to other views of reality. We forget that the paradigm formed from our experience with the world is not etched in granite. It should be more like a form in sand that can shift with the winds. It is a liberating experience to be able to see things in ways we would never see with our current paradigms.

With paradigms we often see what we expect to see—it is selective perception. As they say, *if you only have a hammer, everything starts to look like a nail*. A small hope we should always entertain is: *let my competitors be content with their paradigms*. When the world changes, they will miss it. It explains why some organizations are left behind when priorities and the delivery of value shift. The world of mainframe computers dissolved into the world of personal computers. The world of large cars dissolved into the world of smaller, more fuel-efficient ones. In each case and many similar ones, successful companies lost their competitive edge because they continued to see and interpret the world through the paradigms of their experience, regardless of how blatant the contrary evidence seems to someone on the outside. Paradigms of competitors and other players in one's industry become the prevailing wisdom. You can find breakthroughs to new levels of understanding by seeing possibilities to shift industry paradigms. If your competitors view the prevailing industry paradigms as unalterable truth, you have the potential for strategic opportunities by breaking the bonds of the old paradigms, seeing things the rest of the industry ignores, operating from a different paradigm, and creating a new reality.

The situation is a little different with customers. If we shift thinking among paradigms before our customers do, we may see possibilities they miss. When customers see the world only in terms of mainframe computers or large cars, there will be a challenge. Their paradigms must shift in order for them to appreciate a different product or service. We do not really care if the paradigms of our competitors shift; the longer they remain with old paradigms, the better off we are. The longer customers remain with old paradigms, the harder it is to bring something new into a business. Understanding paradigms that customers and others hold is a powerful competitive advantage. It is not a simple task; we cannot observe paradigms directly.

Laying the Groundwork (Perceiving)

We can observe the frequent result of paradigms: behavioral patterns—what different players or the entire industry seems to do on a regular basis. The thinking process on detecting patterns—Chapter 14—may have all the information we need for this phase of the thinking process. The first approach in that chapter for perceiving patterns was identifying typical key events or activities; this is a good way to get the insight needed to describe the behavioral patterns. There are several pattern categories to consider, such as:

- Competitor response to changing market conditions.
- Competitor initiatives to change strategy, enter new markets, retain old markets, or introduce new products.
- Customer response to different products and marketing techniques.
- Customer buying habits and the product expectations they have held.
- Strategies, initiatives, and typical activities of suppliers, distributors, and producers of complementary products in running their businesses.
- Typical events in the industry as it grows, matures, and declines.
- Stated thinking of different environment participants in company reports, business magazines, and so on.

Seeing the Value (Understanding)

Our goal here is clear: understand the paradigms that inhibit the thinking of competitors and others in the industry and the paradigms of customers with which we will have to contend. As you look at these paradigms, recognize three things. They are there for a reason because they facilitate some actions and decisions. They also constrain other actions and decisions. They also cause us never to see some things. We frequently experience these three categories as allowing us to maintain efficient operations, constraining us from experimenting with operational changes that would increase effectiveness, and failing to entertain ideas that would require new operations and make the current ones obsolete.

We now have the rather difficult task of determining paradigms that consistently explain those past behavioral patterns and will probably help predict future behavior. It is a more intuitive process to identify alternative ideas for paradigms; we rely more on logic to test them against the evidence of the observable patterns. Even with logic, we may not be certain that we have correctly identified the paradigm and risk being incorrect. Acting only on observation of behavioral patterns without using intuition to surmise the underlying paradigm also carries risk. Decide which risk you are willing to accept.

Coca-Cola and Pepsi have been locked in a long-term struggle. The introduction of *New Coke* reflected a view of behavioral patterns only—consumers bought each product on the basis of taste. Duplicate the taste of the competitor and it is possible to take additional market share. There seems to have been a small paradigm operating that worked against the new product introduction but was also a positive reflection on Coca-Cola in the first place—a belief that the brand name reflected a tradition, in its *secret* formula and taste, that was worth keeping. If they had understood this paradigm prior to the new product introduction, they might have reconsidered and saved money.

A clue to determining paradigms may come from Chapter 16. We had one approach where we looked at the potential for a shock wave to overthrow things that we take for granted. It is commonplace to depend upon things that fall from view because they do not seem central to the business' operation and people do not believe those things will change. It is easy to point out problems in the closing days of the big car era, but the long years of inexpensive gasoline probably created a paradigm in thinking that inhibited design preparation for alternative vehicles. See if behavioral patterns you identified reflect this tendency to take things for granted. Decide whether that kind of oversight leads to a paradigm.

Another clue may come from a connection to priorities. How do businesses form paradigms? It seems that some come from the behavioral pattern of responding to customer priorities even if the business influenced those priorities in the first place. It would not be surprising if Apple had shared a paradigm with IBM about the viability of mainframes in business. Perhaps this came from seeing the customer priorities for computing power and centralized operations. This paradigm seems to have caused a delayed entry into personal computers by IBM and may have caused Apple to miss early positioning for business purchases of personal computers. These purchases led to a new priority—compatibility between home and office—that affected Apple's target market. TV networks may have believed that a priority they helped create—free television programming—became a paradigm; people will never pay for something they can get for free. Although Federal Communications Commission (FCC) regulations may have inhibited expansion by networks, this paradigm led to discounting the threat from cable TV and pay-per-view operations.

Customer priorities, which are observable in their purchase behavior patterns, frequently originate in customer paradigms. This may reveal why some priorities are easier to change than others. A strategy to shift priorities may require deliberate action to shift paradigms or blend with paradigms that are not changing. To say that some paradigms can shift and others may be relatively impervious to change implies that not all paradigms are the same. We know that we are often unaware of our own paradigms and it is possibly correct that we do not change what we cannot see. Paradigms exist in our thinking at different levels. The deeper a paradigm exists in a person's thinking, the more difficult it will be to change it. Following are four very broad levels of paradigms; there is a clear distinction among them.

At the first level are paradigms about a particular industry and its products. You can see this for yourself by picking any product you buy and thinking of paradigms you hold directly related to that product. For example, do you have a different belief about the quality, handling, or performance of American cars versus foreign cars? In basic consumer products, do you believe that brand names imply a different standard than generic names? Do you believe that technological changes in sporting goods—skis, tennis rackets, golf clubs—lead to noticeable differences in performance? Whether you answer *yes* or *no* to these questions, it should be clear that we operate from some paradigms directly related to products. These types of paradigms are changeable; that does not mean that it will be easy for a business to shift them.

The next three levels are different from the first. They represent increasingly greater levels of abstraction from our focus on business and strategy. They may even seem unnecessary at first because we are going to levels that are deeper in a person's thinking and increasingly impervious to change. Maybe everything is subject to change—check your own paradigm on that one—but they are unlikely to shift as a result of the action of a single organization. These levels have strategic importance that we will pick up in the reasoning phase of this thinking process.

The next level is more general, including paradigms about how to organize things so that they function more effectively. Beliefs about hierarchical, centralized, decentralized, networked, and matrix organizational structures fall into this level. Beliefs about teamwork, bureaucracy, and committees are in this level as well. Political beliefs such as democracy, equality, and private property seem to be on the deeper, more fundamental side of this level.

The third level reflects paradigms about people. These include beliefs about raising children and the role of the family. It includes beliefs about individualism, personal responsibility, fairness, and freedom. It includes beliefs about whether or not people are basically good or evil, whether people can be trusted or not, whether people will act according to ethics and principles or need rules to control their behavior. The paradigms of different cultures also exist at this level.

The fourth level is somewhat more fundamental. Joseph Jaworski, in his book *Synchronicity: The Inner Path of Leadership*, talks about the contrast between a main traditional view as seeing everything as a world of things with seeing it as a world of relationships. Margaret Wheatley, in her book *Leadership and the New Science*, writes about a similar comparison between the Newtonian mechanistic view of the world and the alternative living systems view of the world. The contrasting world views in both books are very similar to the complementary thought modes we spoke of in Chapter 6. This is equivalent to looking at thinking trapped in one combination—analytic, divided, and sequential. The contrasting modes—synthetic, holistic, and simultaneous—are a completely different world view. It becomes a deeply embedded paradigm when thinking never enters a complementary mode. The other thought mode pairs may also reveal something about paradigms at this level: logic and intuition, convergence and divergence, hierarchy and network. The hopes and fears about the future that we addressed in scenario planning can also exist in paradigms at this level. It is often a fundamental paradigm to look at the future as filled with promise, progress, and opportunities in contrast to hazards and problems.

Moving Forward (Reasoning)

The last chapter included a long list of opportunities, threats, and constraints that led to strategic possibilities involving the delivery of value to satisfy priorities. The first thing you would want to do is see if those ideas involve the need to shift any paradigms. If so, consider how you would modify those possibilities to enable the shift in paradigms.

The next point to consider is the influence of alternative futures on paradigms. Do the scenarios you articulated, including the most likely case, depend upon different paradigms from the present? If so, it is important to understand how paradigms will shift in order for those scenarios to be plausible. Do trends in different environmental forces lead to new paradigms? One thing about pervasive technological change is that it eventually causes paradigms to shift—consider the impact of the automobile age and the information age on how we think about things as well as what we do. These may be gradual changes but it is important to recognize the shift taking place in paradigms as it is happening. Shock waves make sudden changes that can jolt paradigms; old paradigms no longer seem relevant. As you consider these alternative futures, influenced by forces outside your control, identify the opportunities, threats, and constraints you face. Define the strategic possibilities that these open for you.

The rest of this section looks at additional strategic possibilities you may spot through looking at the world through the idea of paradigms people hold rather than their priorities. Spotting additional strategic possibilities revolves around a single question—*can we shift paradigms to our competitive advantage?* We can answer this question in three different ways: for ourselves, for other players in the industry, and for customers. Let's start with the easiest answer—*yes*, if we mean our own paradigms. Having the fluidity of thinking to see the world through different paradigms, especially the ones I labeled as being at a deeper level, is an achievement. Talking about the topic only makes us aware of the challenge. If the chapter creates nothing more than an ability to articulate your own paradigms, seeing what they help and hinder, it will be a big step in the right direction. From that basis alone you can see strategic possibilities you may have missed. If that ability leads to an appreciation for the value of other paradigms, it will open even more possibilities. Your own behavioral patterns may be easy to spot from thoughts such as we're doing things this way because we have always done them that way. You want to look at paradigms you hold at all four levels. Shifting to alternative paradigms is analogous to one of the major things we do in creative thinking—becoming more creative by removing blocks to our thinking.

The next answer to the question is a little more challenging—*maybe*, if we mean the paradigms held by others in the industry. Early in the chapter I said that one great hope would be to have competitors enamored of their own paradigms as they would then fail to see opportunities we could spot. This is a fortuitous start; it is not the strategy itself. If your competitors hold the paradigm, it could be that all other players also hold it as true—*the prevailing industry wisdom.* Think of the resistance you would offer to someone taking action in a way that contradicted one of the paradigms you held about your business. It is certainly an advantage to see things that others miss, but your strategy may need to accommodate the resistance you will meet as you try to shift paradigms. Shifting paradigms is not a philosophical exercise; it occurs because you intend to do something that currently does not exist, such as offering new products or services, delivering value in a new way, forming relationships or partnerships with different players. Any strategic possibility you identify that shifts paradigms is something the goes against industry norms. You should be testing for paradigms about industry norms at all four levels.

As you consider alternative paradigms, identify the opportunities, threats, and constraints they would pose for your organization, competitors, suppliers, distributors, providers of complementary products, and strategic partners. It may be that by using alternative paradigms you will discover possibilities that do not require an actual shift in the industry norms. In that case, you would see things others miss without doing things that create resistance. On the other hand, some of the possibilities you list may depend upon other players not shifting their paradigms because you are hoping their thinking remains blocked, which delays their following your lead. Finally, you may discover that some of your strategic possibilities depend upon some industry norms staying in place; if another player causes a paradigm shift, it will work to your disadvantage.

The last answer to the question—*can we shift paradigms to our competitive advantage?*—is more interesting. If we are talking about customers, particularly those we label consumers, we can shift paradigms at the surface level but not the ones at the deeper level. What we can do is *shift our thinking about paradigms.* We can shape strategic possibilities that leverage from the deeply embedded ones. Paradigms reveal what people really care about. Those deeper paradigms affect purchase decisions and help explain why certain priorities are fairly stable. It is easy to see how paradigms about raising children or the role of the family appear in a range of decisions such as family vacations, toys, educational software, home computers, home security, and car safety features. Obviously, product promotion ideas would stress the connection to those deeper paradigms, but I am emphasizing something different here. By looking at those paradigms, can you identify substantively different strategic possibilities from the ones you saw by looking at priorities and values? By working with these deeper paradigms, can you alter the more surface level paradigms related to particular industries or products? By thinking about these paradigms, can you create different priorities related to your products or services?

Think about how the paradigms held in the United States about individualism and personal freedom come out in the number of single-occupant vehicles clogging the roads, the number of four-wheel-drive sport utility vehicles that never leave urban areas, the use of the Internet, and the ownership of a wide range of appliances and tools that have very limited use and would be cheaper to rent when needed.

The point of these thoughts is that opportunities exist to tie in to deeper paradigms. Threats exist if competitors are better able to recognize the power of these deeper paradigms than you are. Constraints exist if you try to move in a strategic direction that will ultimately confront one of these paradigms. Remember that people do not need to be aware of their own paradigms in order to act from them.

CHAPTER 20

Doing What You Must—
Selecting Critical Success Factors

Initial Thoughts

The essence of this process is leveraging critical success factors to one's competitive advantage.

Critical success factors provide a third major perspective for gaining competitive advantage. Critical success factors are items that help determine who will prevail on the competitive field. Therefore, they identify what you must manage well in order to succeed. There is admirable clarity to the Federal Express slogan—*when it absolutely, positively has to be there overnight.* We could call a critical success factor anything you *absolutely, positively* must mange to survive and thrive in an industry. More than that, however, their slogan reflects critical success factors. What are the things they need to manage well in order to deliver on the slogan's promise? They have critical success factors regarding pickup, delivery, transportation between sites, and widespread coverage. Their slogan also defined the industry and becomes the obvious standard for others to meet in order to compete successfully. Overnight delivery service does not mean very much if a company is unable to meet its guarantee. Prior to Federal Express, overnight delivery had been an unmet priority. There were probably shipping industry paradigms about the impossibility of meeting that priority. Critical success factors amplify the strategy that has its roots in delivering value to satisfy customer priorities.

Competing companies frequently select different critical success factors to distinguish themselves from each other. Some important factors become the minimum stakes for even participating in the industry. For example, if every organization is creating quality products, it is not possible to gain competitive advantage by emphasizing quality. Quality is a minimum necessity to survive within the industry. If you follow the evolution of any industry you will quickly see that new critical success factors that give some organizations competitive advantage gradually become the necessary entry qualifications. When it is a minimum standard, it remains in the forefront of people's awareness and requires deliberate effort to meet it.

Dell Computer demonstrates the use of critical success factors in their logistics management. An April 7, 1997 *Business Week* article praised their inventory and production systems. Dell has chosen to focus their strategy on mail, phone, and web orders. They use speed as a critical success factor to turn what is often a low margin business, especially in a crowded market such as personal computers, into one that generates high profits while offering high service to customers. Speed is achieved in several ways. They include the entire supply chain in their just-in-time processes. When they receive a computer order they e-mail United Parcel Service, who times the delivery of the computer and monitor to the customer's location. Dell never sees or handles the monitor by using this multi-point supply for single-point delivery method. They even use electronic commerce so their sales become cash to them within 24 hours.

Volvo chose to emphasize safety as their critical success factor. They led the industry in certain innovations. As many of these features become requirements, they still occupy people's attention as minimum standards for being in the industry but become less of a distinctive factor for Volvo. As time goes on, however, they gradually fade into the background. They become so deeply ingrained that they no longer require conscious thought and are just part of normal operations. Safety glass and seat belts have been minimum standards for so long that they are no longer mentioned. They are as much a part of the vehicle as the tires. Over time, other features such as antilock brakes, dual airbags, and side impact bags will follow the same path. It will be increasingly difficult for Volvo to find safety-related critical success factors to distinguish itself from its competitors.

Industries continue to evolve in this way. Therefore, we can look at critical success factors as a sequence.

- The current minimum standards necessary to remain in the industry that may reflect former critical success factors.
- The current critical success factors that companies select to gain competitive advantage.
- The current critical success factors that will become minimum standards as the industry evolves.
- The critical success factors that will become the new grounds for competitiveness as the industry evolves.
- The critical success factors that can be brought into existence by the action of your organization.

- The critical success factors that can be brought into existence by the action of your competitors.

Former critical success factors that have moved through the minimum standard category to the regular part of normal operations phase do not require any strategic thought. This process of evolution tells us something quite interesting: if you identify a critical success factor that really distinguishes you from your competition, do not expect to have that advantage forever. There are only two alternatives: competitors try to copy you or they do not. If they do not, it probably means that the industry is evolving in another direction and your critical success factors will not become minimum standards. They will become irrelevant to the industry.

Laying the Groundwork (Perceiving)

In identifying critical success factors, it is best to start with what we already have done. We have identified many strategic possibilities by looking at priorities and the delivery of value. Some of these factors are then easy to state—*what does the company need to do to use the opportunities, meet the threats, and manage the constraints that it sees in delivering value to satisfy priorities*? Take the ideas generated in Chapter 18 and identify factors your organization must manage to support its focus on value delivery. What you will find is that many of these factors relate to items internal to the operation of the organization such as manufacturing or personnel issues. Other factors may relate to relationships with other players such as securing a steady flow of critical supplies. The customers experience the results of your successfully managing these factors.

We can make similar statements about critical success factors necessary to support strategic possibilities raised by looking at shifting paradigms. Are there critical success factors you must manage to keep your organization able to think through different paradigms? The way you conduct meetings and include different people's thinking may become a critical success factor. Are there critical success factors you must manage to shift paradigms within the industry? The way you provide support to your partners, suppliers, distributors, or providers of complementary products to make the necessary adaptations to remain successful when paradigms shift may become a critical success factor. Are there critical success factors you must manage to shift customer paradigms or leverage from their more deeply held paradigms?

Minimum standards are former critical success factors that every company must meet. If there are alternative ways to operate to those standards, there may be additional terrain for critical success factors. For example, quality—usually in the form of low defect rates and reliability—has become increasingly important to many manufacturers. The various methods used to attain quality standards will often contain choices about critical success factors.

There is one other category to consider in this phase. It seems entirely within reason to consider profit an important part of success. Therefore, we want to include an important category of critical success factors—what drives revenues and costs. We are seeking to manage those factors most connected to generating revenue and those most connected to controlling significant costs. For example, many restaurants make significant portions of their profit from liquor sales. The costs often come from rent, food, and personnel. Restaurant strategy, however, focuses on the type of restaurant, the dining experience, the choice of menu, and the target market. Therefore, restaurants have critical success factors related to revenue and cost drivers that are not central to their strategic possibilities, the value they deliver, or paradigms. The strategy revolves around attracting customers to the restaurant; revenue and cost drivers relate to extracting money once they are there. In Chapter 18 we said that the prime business focus should be on maximizing the delivery of value rather than maximizing profit. There is nothing contradictory here. Profitability is the reward the business seeks—*how do we benefit from the value we create for others?*

There are, therefore, four types of critical success factors to identify in this phase, those that:

- Support your ability to use strategic possibilities related to delivering value.
- Support your ability to use strategic possibilities related to shifting paradigms.
- Enable you to meet minimum industry standards.
- Generate revenue and control costs.

To get a fuller picture of the current situation, identify critical success factors used by your competitors in those four categories.

Seeing the Value (Understanding)

Customers will experience many critical success factors directly. For example, in purchasing software, customers have the obvious priority of easily using it for their needs. Often they expect support in the form of documentation and technical staff. Therefore, critical success factors for the software producer obviously include the quality of documentation writers, training of technical staff, and operations that make it easy for customers to get help through telephone, fax, or e-mail. Think of similar critical success factors you must manage. In this example, perhaps in your own case as well, the need for these critical success factors reveals an entirely different opportunity. These critical success factors are there only because there is no other apparent solution to the problem of effectively using complex software. Sometimes these factors are compensations for problems we have in delivering value for the original customer priority. We might try to find better ways of satisfying the priority and eliminate the need for compensating critical success factors altogether.

The next area to consider is the influence of the industry's evolution on critical success factors. Let's look at the software example again. Part of the need for the support relates to the technical sophistication of the user. We are in the early stages of the personal computer industry. As people gain more knowledge and experience, they do not have the same needs for support. There is no doubt that children growing up using computers have different capabilities than adults. This is a longer term evolution in that industry where the critical success factors necessary for one group of consumers will be different from those for another group. The situation is similar, however, for any industry in which customers and other players grow with their experience. Think about how this type of evolution will alter the need for critical success factors identified in the perceiving phase of the process. This evolution means that formerly important critical success factors are no longer important; they have not become minimum standards. They fade from view because they are not relevant to emerging market conditions.

Our alternative views of the future—scenarios, shock waves, and trends in environmental forces—also reveal changes in critical success factors. Each of these futures can alter patterns, priorities, and paradigms leading to the need for different critical success factors. Perhaps they cause some critical success factors to become minimum standards and others to fade away in importance. At the same time, they open the possibility for new critical success factors.

Moving Forward (Reasoning)

Opportunities exist if the changing nature of the industry opens possibilities for your business to introduce new critical success factors. Opportunities exist if your business can select critical success factors that create a distinctive competitive advantage. Opportunities exist if another company introduces new critical success factors that you are able to duplicate.

Threats exist if the changing nature of the industry opens possibilities for other businesses to introduce new critical success factors that work to your disadvantage. Threats exist when other businesses follow your critical success factors and you begin to lose your distinctive competitive advantage. Threats exist if other businesses introduce critical success factors that begin to make the ones you selected irrelevant to success.

Constraints exist if the changing nature of the industry or actions by other players make it difficult for you to use your critical success factors. This happens when you are dependent upon the actions of others. Companies are dependent upon the actions of providers of complementary products to aid their generation of revenue. Similarly, retail stores often depend upon actions of nearby retailers influencing the location's attractiveness to consumers.

Although critical success factors are an important aspect of competitive advantage, they are often not in the center of strategy. As we saw in the perceiving phase, many of these factors support the initiatives you choose to pursue in delivering value or shifting paradigms. These factors also focus on the revenue and cost drivers that extract profits from following those initiatives. Critical success factors also illuminate the dynamic nature of any business; nothing is permanent. It almost has the feeling of the market saying—*what have you done for us lately*? Today's advantage may not become tomorrow's disadvantage, but there is an ongoing need to reinvent one's business. More than anything, these factors focus attention on a few things that will really matter to success. It is not that they give the company license to do other things poorly; they form the nuclei for these other actions. They help the business know where to allocate its resources, where it will get the best return for its effort.

North Face is one of the more respected names in sleeping bags, packs, tents, and clothing for mountaineering and skiing to deal with the challenges of weather and other demanding conditions. Their products are more expensive than most alternatives. They try to stay in the forefront of innovative design for the targeted activities by using high-quality materials that match the harshest conditions one might experience. A tent designed to survive an expedition to Mount Everest is the same one people buy for summer backpacking trips in the United States. Although competing goods may serve many people as well, the attraction to people is that their merchandise is built to last. There are several critical success factors in this example, but the one that is probably most interesting is their unconditional lifetime guarantee. (I suppose complete misuse such as running a knife through the fabric or dropping the merchandise in a campfire would invalidate this guarantee.) They are willing to bear the expense as the selection of this critical success factor creates an image of the products that adds an extra piece of competitive distinctiveness.

When RCA had color television technology, they chose to license manufacturing of TV sets in order to create a market for the cameras they would sell to studios and television stations. They did not believe they could succeed in holding a monopoly position and get the market to grow at a sufficient rate. Similarly, Netscape gave away thousands of Internet browser programs. In both cases there was a clear focus on a critical success factor of widespread distribution to establish a market presence and create an installed base. They were both willing to take steps, which appear unusual at first glance, to make this critical success factor effective and pave the way for other products for their profitability.

Critical success factors do not always require unusual actions. To work, however, they frequently require dedicated focus. They are not gimmicks. In many cases such as the examples above, the company must be willing to sacrifice something or take some risk to make it work.

Matching Levers with Capabilities

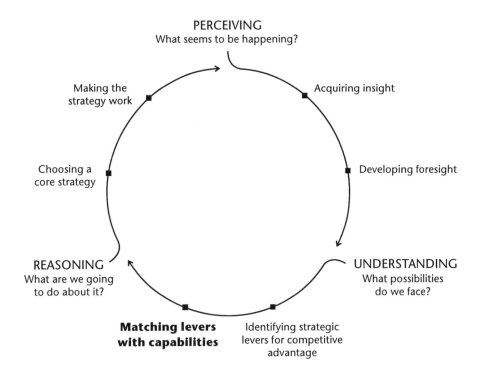

CHAPTER 21

Balancing Offense and Defense

Initial Thoughts

The essence of this process is matching strengths and weaknesses to strategic possibilities.

What do we need to do to take advantage of the strategic possibilities? We need to match them to strengths the organization currently has and strengths it could build to determine its initiatives for the future—its offensive moves. At the same time it needs to use its current and developing strengths and protect its weaknesses to deal with the strategic possibilities that others grasp—its defensive moves. Throughout the last three chapters we have identified strategic possibilities for delivering value, shifting paradigms, and selecting critical success factors. We organized these into opportunities, threats, and constraints. Let's briefly revisit these three terms.

Opportunities mean greater degrees of freedom, increased likelihood of growth or expansion, and additional influence for the company. As the environment changes, opportunities open. A company can create its own opportunities by seeing things overlooked by competitors or by increasing the opportunities or reducing the threats or constraints faced by their customers, suppliers, distributors, or strategic partners. They also create opportunities by erecting threats or constraints for their competitors. Opportunities are temporal in nature; combinations of favorable circumstances will not exist in perpetuity. The company must act or watch the opportunity evaporate.

Threats mean diminished degrees of freedom, increased likelihood of contraction, and reduced influence for the company. As the environment changes, threats appear. Actions by competitors or other players can increase the number or intensity of threats it faces. Threats are temporal; it may be possible to wait them out, but any threat, whether responded to or not, can have devastating consequences for the company. An opportunity can become a threat if you do not have the means to tap it or if your competitor chooses it.

Constraints are boundaries or restraints on intended actions. They hold the company in its current position or inhibit it from taking a new position. As the environment changes, constraints can grow or diminish. Constraints may be temporal, but waiting them out means forgoing the intended action.

We approach opportunities, threats, and constraints with our strengths and weaknesses. What is a strength? What is a weakness? Try a simple exercise by making a list of your personal strengths and weaknesses. Your strength list probably contains knowledge, skills, abilities, and other personal qualities. Your list of weaknesses probably contains things you feel you could improve. To some extent the list does not mean very much standing by itself. It needs a context. In creating the list you may have thought about where you have been more or less successful. That is a context. You may have thought about work, home, interests or hobbies, and other experiences. These provide context. If someone asks you to head up a task force, some strengths become important and others are irrelevant. Weaknesses may or may not matter to that particular job. If you are responsible for creating a new product, managing a children's sports team, or planning a vacation, the relevant strengths and weaknesses obviously shift. A strength is a strength only if it matters in a particular context. A weakness is a weakness only if it hinders you in a particular context.

It is similar for a business; it makes no sense simply to list its strengths and weaknesses in isolation from a meaningful context. We have been creating that type of context through the entire flow of strategic thought. We have looked at the changing shape of forces and players, patterns, scenarios, and shock waves to acquire insight into the business and develop foresight about alternative futures. In each of those processes we also thought about how the firm could respond to the changing course of events. We were casting this widening and deepening net on the environment to expand the range of strategic possibilities. We were moving from the environment to the company. We never, however, addressed its specific strengths or weaknesses. As we moved through the three strategic levers we brought additional focus to this external view by finding specific strategic possibilities. Even at this point we did not focus on strengths and weaknesses.

A strength is something you can capitalize on for strategies or actions that give you the ability to take opportunities, resist threats, and face constraints. A company must have some advantage and must have it for something that matters. A business's strengths tend to result from past successful activities or strategic initiatives. For example, a company does R&D resulting in patents. The patents then become a strength for future actions. The patents also reflect a strength in technological capability. In the last chapter an example about software pointed to documentation writers and technical staff as a critical success factor. Depending upon how the market changes, these personnel capabilities may not be strengths for future decisions. If the industry evolves to user-friendly software or more sophisticated customers, these capabilities will no longer be a strength. Strengths include a wide range of additional company resources, capabilities, and characteristics such as cash position, brand names, location, contracts, partnerships and alliances, breadth of product line, breadth of market experience including global operations, production processes and technology, company culture, typical management processes, market share, and loyalty of customers.

A weakness is something that reduces the chances of exploiting opportunities, intensifies the consequences of threats, or makes constraints nearly insurmountable. Given the list of possible company strengths, a weakness may be nothing more than the absence of a strength in a critical area. Current weaknesses often derive from things not needed in the past; there was no reason to develop a particular strength so there was no effort or investment to build a strength. As the industry evolves, those things previously omitted may become important for success. There will always be some weaknesses, so we often use strengths in one area to compensate for weaknesses in another.

Given these views of strengths and weaknesses, our task should be relatively straightforward. Create a summary of all the opportunities, threats, and constraints identified from the previous thinking processes. Match that summary with relevant company strengths and weaknesses to determine the best choices for strategy—which opportunities the firm will pursue, how it will prepare to deal with threats, and how it will overcome constraints.

Laying the Groundwork (Perceiving)

The summary and matching process above are the first steps of this thinking process. The following is a quick review of some of the main categories for opportunities, threats, and constraints identified for the strategic levers in the thinking processes of the last three chapters.

Opportunities
- Opening in the future to expand your delivery of value or make it more distinctive and attain a more secure position
- Environmental changes that directly shift paradigms or create openings for you to shift paradigms to your advantage
- Evolution of the business that allows new critical success factors that work to your advantage

Threats
- Actions by players or changes in forces that can diminish your delivery of value
- Environmental changes that directly shift paradigms or create openings for others to shift paradigms to your disadvantage

- Evolution of the business that allows others to introduce critical success factors that work to your disadvantage

Constraints

- Anything in the environment that severely restrains your ability to deliver value
- Existing paradigms that are resistant to change and constrain your initiatives
- Evolution of the industry or actions of other players that hinder your use of selected critical success factors

It is possible that you noticed other opportunities, threats, and constraints working on the business field map, environmental force trends, in-depth understanding of players, patterns, scenarios, and shock waves, but cannot draw a connection to the strategic levers—delivering value, shifting paradigms, and selecting critical success factors. Include these in your summary as well.

The next step is matching strengths and weaknesses with the opportunities, threats, and constraints. There are two slightly different ways to approach this. In the first method, take each opportunity, threat, and constraint and assess which company resources, capabilities, or characteristics are relevant strengths to place the company in the best position. Also determine what the company lacks—its weaknesses. You are determining which company strengths makes it best able to exploit an opportunity, counter a threat, and manage a constraint. You are also assessing which weaknesses makes the company more vulnerable.

The second method is to think about what kind of strength would be best to take advantage of the opportunity, counter the threat, or overcome the constraint. Then determine whether the company possesses it or lacks it. This is a way of asking which strength is needed to exploit an opportunity and which weakness would make a company particularly vulnerable to a threat or ineffective in the face of a constraint. Obviously, the company would want to consider building the needed strengths.

Seeing the Value (Understanding)

This flow of thought from the environment to specific opportunities, threats, and constraints to a match with the company's strengths and weaknesses appears logical but is not an entirely accurate representation of reality. The whole time that we were thinking about the environment and its future possibilities we were probably looking at it through the view of our own strengths and weaknesses. For example, if someone comes up to us and says, *I've got a great opportunity for you*, we become cautious. We may realize that an opportunity exists only if we have the strengths or desire to take advantage of it. Otherwise, it is not an opportunity. It may even be a threat if someone else has the appropriate strength. As we look at the environment, alternative futures, and strategic levers, we may see opportunities, threats, and constraints through the filters of our own strengths and weaknesses.

We can see that the relatively sequential line of thought we believed we were following dissolves once we talk explicitly about strengths and weaknesses; it is more simultaneous. We can be somewhat objective in trying to identify opportunities, threats, and constraints, but our view often depends upon the current state of company resources, capabilities, and characteristics. It is important to strive for the more objective view. Opportunities exist in the environment whether we are able to take advantage of them or not. If we look at the environment only through the filter of our own strengths and weaknesses we will miss what is really happening. Check your own list to see if you managed to keep the opportunities, threats, and constraints relatively objective—a reflection of the changing environment—or if your list tended to a more subjective side.

Opportunities are like an orchard of ripe apples. If we pass them by or are unable to reach them, they may not look like an opportunity. Someone else, however, may be in a better position to take advantage. Similarly, people from different companies with the same strategic thinking may see different things, filtered by the strengths and weaknesses they possess. They have different strengths so they tend to see different opportunities; different weaknesses lead to different threats. As an opportunity to one can be a threat to another, relative strengths and weaknesses also become an issue. Moves by others that expose weaknesses or open new weaknesses may also reduce the significance of one's strengths. How do you stack up against competitors for the different opportunities? What do they have that you lack? What do you have that they lack? Given the environment and their strengths, what could they do that becomes a threat because you lack the appropriate strength? In playing chess it is quite risky to hope an opponent misses an opportunity. Playing the game by counting on someone else's ignorance is unreasonable. If there is an opportunity in the environment and you are unable to move, then it is useful to figure out how your competitors might move.

Timing, therefore, is the third issue to look at in addition to the first two above: maintaining a relatively objective view and getting a sense of relative strengths and weaknesses. We want to look at the time frame for these opportunities, threats, and constraints—how long they will have an effect, how long they will be valid, and how long you will have to act. It also useful to get a sense of the necessary timing to take maximum advantage of the opportunities or minimize the effects of threats or constraints. When we think of a window of opportunity, do we mean that it just closes or that someone else has moved faster to exploit it?

Moving Forward (Reasoning)

As we match the array of opportunities, threats, and constraints with strengths and weaknesses, we clearly miss opportunities, have difficulty warding off threats, and get stopped by constraints because we lack certain strengths. We are not who we are forever; the changing environment may alert us to strengths we need to develop in order to alter our position. Similarly, when competitors have a relative strength for worthwhile opportunities or the timing requires different strengths, we have signs of the need to develop new strengths. What options do we face for this challenge? As the future unfolds and we see which strengths become necessary, how do we get them? We said strengths tend to be a result of success in previous actions or strategies; we learn by doing. If so, we need a plan to develop the strengths in the organization in time to move on the opportunity or meet the threat. The other route, of course, is to buy the strength through hiring people, outsourcing, subcontracting, consultants, mergers, acquisitions, or partnerships. Similar options are available if we are trying only to protect a weakness rather than build a new strength.

We practically have a strategy in hand at this point, although I do want to introduce a few other thoughts in the next two chapters before settling on a single path. We can filter from the broader range of possibilities to ones that seem more relevant to the company's present and developable capabilities. We are choosing those opportunities we will most likely pursue. These are opportunities to deliver value, shift paradigms, or select new critical success factors. A strategy is nothing more than balancing the offense and defense. The offensive move is combining a coherent connection among those three levers with present and possible strengths. The defensive move is managing one's vulnerability to threats. To handle constraints we may have ideas for offense—using strengths—and defense—shielding weaknesses. Perhaps as you have been reading this chapter a question has been floating in the back of your mind. Can we make our own future? It sounds as if we have been responding to the environment. The basic approach has been matching one's strengths and weaknesses to conditions we believe will exist in the environment. Are we doomed always to be in a reactive mode? I would not call it reactive, as we are taking a forward view. Can we create our own opportunities? We'll continue this theme in the next chapter.

CHAPTER 22

Playing Your Best Hand

Initial Thoughts

The essence of this process is deriving strategic possibilities from the collective capability of the company's personnel.

As we were developing different scenarios about the future and considered different shock waves, what were we thinking? Do we have the alternative future views as a means of dealing with our uncertainty? Only one future is going to happen. Although we tend to plan for the most likely scenario, we do not know which future will occur. We need to explore several alternative futures in order to prepare ourselves in case we guessed wrong. A different perspective is that the alternative futures are real possibilities. Therefore, by our action we can tip the balance in one direction or another. That is, the future is open for our choosing. We know that different products have shifted society—the automobile, the computer, and now, probably, the Internet. Clearly, all the companies in these industries have created a different future by their actions. Did they simply grasp an opportunity that was lying there untapped? They shaped technology and products to meet significant priorities that were insufficiently satisfied. At the same time they certainly shifted paradigms. Did they, therefore, create their own opportunity?

Maybe it seems that this is just some philosophical musing about the future. There is an important difference between the two views—choosing a path in the presence of our uncertainty about possible futures versus acting to influence the future that does arrive. We have been following a path related to the first view, which I would label *outside-in*, shifting our thinking from an understanding of the environment and projection of alternative futures to an array of opportunities. The next step was using relevant current and developable strengths to decide which opportunities to pursue for the company's advantage. From what is available to us, we decide what to become. The other view, influencing the future, I would label *inside-out*. We start from who we are or are trying to become and try to shape a future to match.

The two views seem contradictory. Fortunately, life is sufficiently complex that we do not need to fall into either-or thinking and decide which is right. We can use both views to the benefit of our own strategic choice. We know that some things are barely influenced by our actions—shock waves and deeply held paradigms, for example. Other things fall well within our influence—evolution of the industry, the birth of new industries, and the surface or product-related paradigms. In the last chapter we briefly visited this inside-out approach by wondering whether our strengths and weaknesses influenced our view of opportunities, threats, and constraints. If we looked at our strengths and sought out opportunities, would we identify different opportunities than we had when the flow of thought started with the environment first? The answer is clearly that we would, which is why strategic thinking is more simultaneous than sequential. The chief purpose of the major strategic thinking cycle is to reinforce this freer flow of thought, beginning at any point and flowing backward or forward on the cycle as necessary. It was never the intention to have your thought locked into a sequential path, regardless of its appealing logic. Therefore, we want to be sure that we take both the outside-in and inside-out views. Why have any chance of missing a beneficial opportunity for the company?

Often, when companies use this inside-out approach they start with their products, trying to determine the best way to position products and capture market share. Even the Boston Consulting Group's useful portfolio approach with stars, dogs, cash cows, and problem children is a product-focused method. A product view is very limited and as restrictive to our thinking as typical industry definitions. We need a more expansive view. If we are starting with the company to look outward, we want to use something more significant that gives us a broader view of the world. Those significant things are the company's key strengths or fundamental capabilities. The most useful contribution to this perspective has come from Gary Hamel and C. K. Prahalad in their *Harvard Business Review* article, "The Core Competence of the Organization," and their book *Competing for the Future*. Incidentally, remember that *competition* and *competency* have the same Latin root of *striving together*. In competition we are striving with other companies, our opponents, to achieve something for customers. In core competency we are striving with others within the company, our colleagues, to achieve something for customers.

To get a first view of this useful concept, list your personal core competencies. In the last chapter, I asked you to list your personal strengths and weaknesses. In contrasting these two experiences most people find that listing strengths and weaknesses feels a little more lighthearted and tends to go rather quickly. Core competency seems more serious. Some people take a while before they respond. We appear to be asking, *who are you*? Strengths and weaknesses seem easier to change; core competency seems much more basic or fundamental. It would take longer to develop. In listing strengths and weaknesses, people typically look at many different contexts. Core competency transcends context in that it is valid in a wide range of different situations. It is similar to core values— the ones we hold as significantly important regardless of the situation. Core values do not change from day to day to suit our mood or circumstances; neither do core competencies. We structure our lives or conduct ourselves in a manner reflecting those core values. Similarly, we are at our best when we can use our core competencies.

When we look at core competencies within a company we get the same kind of picture. They are not easy to identify. Identifying them is a more serious matter than identifying strengths. Core competencies are valid for a variety of situations, products, or industries. They are something upon which the company can build its future. Core competencies are behind the scenes and permeate everything; they are the common thread running through all products. We can build a strategy around core competencies. Customers experience the expression of them in your products. For example, all artists know about paint, canvas, light, form, and so forth, but core competency is what distinguishes Magritte from Monet or Van Gogh. It is not just the style but the ability, attitude, uniqueness, and interpretation of the world that underlies or creates the style. Customers experience the style but it is core competency that creates it.

Perhaps the most important distinction is that core competencies are completely dependent upon people. Strengths can be a variety of other resources and characteristics that we listed in the last chapter, such as financial position, market share, reputation, brand names, and contracts. It is certainly possible that company strengths you identified to meet the opportunities, threats, and constraints in the environment were really core competencies.

The notion of core competency is an extremely useful way of thinking of the organization as possessing some unique set of skills applicable to a wider range of products. Naturally, organizations do not possess skills; they are embedded within the people of the organization. Therefore, the core competency concept also elevates the importance of people as crucial to the strategic future of the organization. For example, biotechnology firms try to develop new products —pharmaceuticals, genetically engineered products, and so on. Focused research skills of the scientists in the organization constitute an important core competency.

Organizations may have many strengths. Core competencies are particular clusters of strengths. A core competency, however, is not simply an inventory of the knowledge and capabilities of its people. It is the collective knowledge and skills of the people, how they are able to work together, and how the organization's structure supports that effort. Each cluster of strengths is really "a bundle of skills and technologies" according to Hamel and Prahalad. The technologies are a major mechanism to organize people's skills. Companies do not randomly hire people and hope that core competencies will evolve from some clever way of blending people with each other. They hire people to fit in and help build core competencies in a particular way. A November 11, 1995 article in *The Economist* viewed it this way, "Core competencies are the flexible skills that allow them to produce a stream of distinctive products that cannot be easily imitated by a rival: miniaturization for Sony, optics for Canon, or timely delivery for Federal Express. . . . Cultivating such skills means putting effort into recruiting and training star employees. . . . Having established what they are good at, learning organizations need to remove internal barriers to the flow of information."

Core competencies, learning organizations, knowledge-creating companies, and intellectual capital are related ideas centering on the collectively organized skills, knowledge, and intelligence of personnel for the company's competitive future. In line with that, there is little doubt that thinking, individually and collectively, should be a core competency for any company. Core competency is a way of focusing a typical listing of strengths into some coherent, market-relevant pattern and identifying the essential nature of the organization that permeates all of its products. It is another way of determining one's competitive advantage, particularly as a base to strategically expand in the future. It creates an integrated coherence of the organization so that it always uses its most important combination of strengths in all of its endeavors.

Laying the Groundwork (Perceiving)

To identify your company's core competencies, first consider personnel skills. The question to ask is, *what is it about our skills that gives us a competitive advantage?* You may have listed these skills as company strengths or capabilities when you worked on the thinking process in the last chapter. A second approach is to consider your current products or services. As you look at them, think about what you do consistently well in creating the products or ensuring that customers receive the value that satisfies their priorities. It is not the product itself but the combined skills of personnel doing something that causes the product to be distinctive from that of competitors. You may have listed these skills when you worked on critical success factors in Chapter 20. For example, when we spoke of Volvo's concentration on safety it is possible that they have a core competency in the design of new safety features. This core competency includes the ability to innovate the features as well as alter the vehicle design and production processes to accommodate the features without significantly increasing costs.

Next, consider the possible core competencies of your competitors. You need to look at their products or services with an admiring rather than critical eye. You need to consider anything you know about their strategy or their operations. The way they position themselves in the market or promote themselves may also give clues to core competencies. It does not matter if the competitors have identified their core competencies. They exist in any company, whether it can see them or not. The real question is whether the company has the competencies that are relevant to the market. Core competencies are something that distinguishes competitors from each other. Look at their competitiveness from the perspective of general personnel skill categories that create their advantage. You are looking for what they do consistently well that delivers value to their customers.

Follow a similar approach to identify core competencies of suppliers, distributors, providers of complementary products, and strategic partners. Trying to see the core competencies of your customers would give you an additional insight into the value they seek. In Chapter 18 we said that their priorities reflect their use of the product or service to create a different product for their customers. From this chapter's perspective we would say that their priorities also relate to products or services that help them refine, develop, or use their core competencies to give them distinctiveness in their products. Consumers or end users are not relevant to this analysis. Although people may think of their individual core competencies, there is probably not much benefit in shaping most products to help them develop or use those competencies. Other than educational products and services, consumers' product use is usually not related to their core competencies.

How many core competencies should you have or be able to see in other players? *Core* means the central, innermost, basic, or most important part, or the essence. That means there should be a small number of distinctive competencies. Hamel and Prahalad say that companies typically have 5 to 15 core competencies; that is an appropriate range to focus upon. They also say the process to identify core competencies in a large company could take months, so recognize the importance of the process. Part of the time results from political maneuvering in the company with people trying to be sure that their skills or areas of expertise and responsibility are part of important core competencies. The main reason for the time is simple: the decision on core competencies is a major determinant of what the company is and will become for several years. For many companies it is also a choice of what they will outsource or subcontract—things that are not core competencies or peripheral to the ones identified. The company will structure itself to operate from its core competencies. Anything else must be a critical support function to those core competencies. It is a choice of its identity. In that manner it is really not different from choosing core values, a vision, a purpose, or the strategy itself—the topics we cover in the next chapter. Will it take months to identify core competencies? That depends on thinking skills, particularly within groups (see Chapter 4).

Seeing the Value (Understanding)

Core competencies must allow extensions beyond the current product offerings. Therefore, it is always a useful exercise to identify additional opportunities you could pursue with core competencies, whether you intend to proceed or not. This small exercise is one of the essential ingredients of this inside-out approach to strategy—defining opportunities based on who you are.

We also know that things change. What is the method for identifying new arenas for core competencies? You really cannot make this choice without considering how your industry seems to be evolving or whether you intend to move into new industries. Seeing some opportunity in the world for which you want to forge a strong market position in an emerging industry also provides insight into new core competencies. Each of these approaches reignites the simultaneous nature of strategic thinking. It is an ongoing process of looking at the environment and then determining what the company needs to do combined with looking at the company and then influencing the environment so the company can successfully do what it chooses.

The final leg of this future view of core competencies is the evolving nature of any industry. In that regard core competencies are similar to critical success factors. There are some that give each company competitive distinctiveness—each company chooses the core competencies that will allow it to succeed. Different companies make different choices. As time goes on, the truly successful core competencies attract imitators and these eventually become minimum standards—the entry ticket to be a player in the industry. As this happens, new core competencies come to the forefront as each company seeks to find its competitive edge. Some former distinctive core competencies may lapse into irrelevance as the industry evolves. With your own distinctive core competencies you are on one of two paths: either other companies will try to duplicate your successes or you are heading down a dead-end street where your competencies will become irrelevant in the future. In either case, it is important to have thinking focused into the future to identify the emerging core competencies. If most of what you identify as your core competencies are fairly widespread among companies in the industry, they are quickly becoming minimum standards. While necessary to maintain and even improve over time, they may not give you enough of a competitive edge.

Moving Forward (Reasoning)

Whether we look at core competencies, strengths, or critical success factors, the company is looking for something to help it get an edge. Other than commodity products, we seek something distinctive in what we sell to customers. We are also saying that the strategy needs to include or even emerge from capabilities that are also distinctive. Strategy is not about momentary uniqueness, which is all one can expect when the whole focus is on the product. Ongoing competitive advantage derives from capabilities. It is capabilities that allow the continuing move into the future, whether it is new products, new markets, product redesigns, or new industries. Product innovations are relatively easy to duplicate. Patents are minor protection. There is a limit to the power of brand loyalty. There are numerous instances of companies with significant financial power losing markets to marginally funded upstarts. It's nice to have money, but nobody believes problems are solved by throwing money at them. Certainly nothing new can be created in this way. All these strengths seem important but they can easily be lost. Other than people leaving the company, we can never lose the collective capabilities of personnel, particularly the capability to think. Even if market evolution renders other core competencies less relevant, the competency to think will enable the company to begin shifting to new core competencies. The core competency to think is fundamental to all others; it is not related to particular markets or industries. It never becomes less relevant. It must be an explicit part of any strategy—unfailing attention to advancing the core competency of thinking.

Core competencies become part of the competitive field. Competition is not confined to the products or services the company sells. It is even more than battle over market share. Capabilities do distinguish products in the present, but a strategic focus on core competency is a launch pad into the future. Therefore, a significant part of competition revolves around building core competencies, being a learning organization, becoming a knowledge-creating company, using intellectual capital, and, as we said, advancing thinking. What is your strategy relative to competitors for bringing people with new talent into the organization, merging them with other people, sustaining a climate that values personnel capability, and forging the collective capabilities needed for the future? Consider the following as part of your strategic thinking for capabilities.

- Training new people to fit in to the existing core competencies. This is not an attempt to have people thinking the same way but a mechanism for effectively benefiting from their knowledge, skills, and intelligence.
- Looking to recruit people who possess the core competencies that seem to be missing in the organization.
- Continuing the development of people to further refine existing core competencies and begin building necessary future competencies.
- Sustaining the organization's structure and culture to support core competencies and make them a central focus around which everything else revolves.

Building new core competencies is a time-consuming process, five to ten years according to Hamel and Prahalad. The time lengthens if the company's structure and culture do not reflect the value of personnel acting collectively. The time lengthens if people have been told, in word or deed, *you're not paid to think*. The time lengthens if measurements and performance appraisals keep people focused on short-term results. The time lengthens if people are overloaded with tasks and goals. The time lengthens if every time the organization suffers a setback it looks to cutting the budget for personnel development or training. The only realistic alternative to internally building a core competency is to merge with another company that already possesses it. A strategic partnership may be a good matching of core competencies with another company, but a failed partnership can cause serious difficulties. Outsourcing and subcontracting for core competencies are even riskier propositions.

There is one other area to consider for strategy around core competencies—the other players on the field. Consider in your strategic choice how you can enable other players to refine and develop their core competencies to use for their competitive advantage. This approach certainly makes you more significant to customers in satisfying their priorities. If your product depends upon complementary products that you have no intention of producing or selling, it is always in your interest to have the providers of these be highly effective companies. Paying attention to these needs may be a way of strengthening strategic partnerships or enhancing relationships with suppliers and distributors.

PART 5

Walking the Talk—
Doing What You Decide

Choosing a Core Strategy

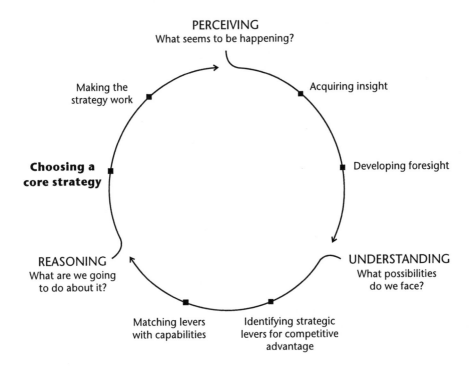

PERCEIVING
What seems to be happening?

Making the
strategy work

Acquiring insight

**Choosing a
core strategy**

Developing foresight

REASONING
What are we going
to do about it?

UNDERSTANDING
What possibilities
do we face?

Matching levers
with capabilities

Identifying strategic
levers for competitive
advantage

CHAPTER 23

Forming the Raison d'Être

Initial Thoughts

The essence of this process is creating a company identity that makes the strategy worth pursuing.

This process is analogous to the denouement of a murder mystery—there are many suspects but only one winds up as the culprit—the strategy. There are many clues—strategic possibilities—that are interesting but do not bear fruit. We probably have the right culprit but we need some finishing touches to be certain we are making the right choice. In the past two chapters we have completed most of the pieces of the puzzle. By matching strengths and weaknesses with opportunities, threats, and constraints and determining core competencies we have what we need for a strategy. In this chapter I want to add a few other aspects of business direction that may create a better sense of the business' identity to shape its strategic choice. The main point to consider in looking at the words in Figure 23–1 is that the only things really necessary are the goals and the strategy. Core values, vision, purpose, and mission are all optional. These ideas have great utility when used well, but there are so many instances of wasted efforts around these topics that I hesitate to speak about them. They have all become fads.

Scott Adams, in his book *The Dilbert Principle*, ridiculed the wasted efforts with this definition of a mission statement: "A long, awkward sentence that demonstrates management's inability to think clearly." He gave this example: "We enhance stock-holder value through strategic business initiatives by empowered employees working in new team paradigms." There is certainly humor in the misguided efforts, but there is also the danger of increased cynicism. When the efforts result in glossy statements that are ultimately meaningless or there is no

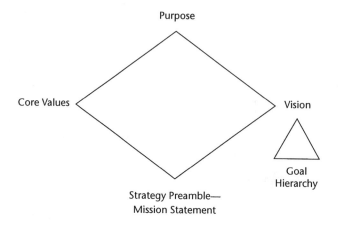

Figure 23–1   The Strategic Decision

real intention to keep them in the forefront of everyone's attention, do not bother creating a mission statement.

My recommendation is simple: be clear about traditional corporate goals such as profit, return on investment, market share, or market growth and how the strategy helps to achieve those goals. Use core values, vision, purpose, and mission *only* if they are clearly and simply stated, absolutely useful to people's energy or focus, and will remain central to ongoing decisions and work. To get this added value, I suggest banning the following words from any value, vision, mission, purpose, or strategy statement: quality, efficiency, effectiveness, empowerment, stakeholders, excellence, world-class, profit or any other word better associated with goals, and critical success factors, core competencies, paradigms, or any words that can seem like jargon. You want to be specific because your company is basically answering the following questions:

- What do we consider essentially important for our strategy and all of our actions?
- What type of future are we excited about and committed to creating?
- Why is that future meaningful to us?
- Why are we in business?
- How are we going to make that future occur?

Seriously answering these questions may be all that is necessary. If an answer seems to be about financial or market achievements, call it a business goal and leave it in that category. We are seeking to determine whether there is any additional power to thoughts beyond goals. Too often, however, we waste time deciding whether we have the correct distinction between values, vision, purpose, and mission. Although I will continue to use these words, the labels are not really important. Thinking is important; fitting thinking into categories is not helpful. If you found the list of questions above worth considering, you could just have one statement labeled, *who we are or what this business is about*. A good answer to any one of those questions may be sufficient to provide additional focus to the necessary use of business goals and strategy. In other words, we can choose to use only values, vision, purpose, or mission; we do not need all four.

I will alter the structure of this chapter a little bit so we can address a complete thinking process for some of the ideas captured in Figure 23–1, with the strategy itself being reserved for the next chapter. First, we'll look at a quick summary of the words. *Core values* are fundamental guidance to all behavior. They are a response to the question, *what do we consider essentially important for our strategy and all of our actions?* A strategy must reflect those values; if it contradicted values, the strategy would be rejected. A *vision* is an image of the future we want to create. It is a response to the question, *what type of future are we excited about and committed to creating?* Obviously, once we consider a vision we are saying that we can influence the future—our inside-out perspective from the last chapter. The *goal hierarchy* represents the flow of desired company achievements from major corporate goals relevant to all activities to goals related to specific tasks. *Purpose* describes what is important about the vision. It is a response to the question, *why is that future, expressed in the vision, meaningful to us?* Or, *why are we in business?* The strategy contains the details of how the company intends to direct its efforts in order to reach the vision. It is a response to the question, *how are we going to make that future occur?* It may contain a preamble of a mission statement that captures the essence of the strategy.

Core Values

Core values create integrity for a company and are analogous to credibility for an individual. They are the foundation of a company's culture. Frequently there are several core values, each one being expressed in very few words. Values are standards or commitments of how people in the company will conduct themselves in dealings with each other and with other organizations. These values will permeate nearly every activity of the company and must guide all efforts directed toward achieving the vision. Values do not change from one situation to another. A company is serious about its values when it keeps them alive in any situation. Values are not sacrificed for expediency. Values are not clever statements emblazoned on posters throughout the company; they are serious elements of guidance.

I have yet to meet an employee of Hewlett-Packard who has not experienced a serious discussion of the H-P Way in the course of some meeting. The guidance embodied in this brief document is not part of every discussion, but people continually refer to it when it is necessary to choose a course of action.

Intel reinforces its values by using them as important dimensions of performance appraisal, noting actions by personnel that reflected the values. Nobody would consider deviating from them. This is not some mechanical adherence to dogma. People do not memorize the H-P Way or any serious set of values and chant them with obeisance. They see the power in coordinating groups of personnel with diverse responsibilities in challenging situations. When we seek shared values, what do we really want? It is not simply agreement with a series of well-meaning statements. It is the commitment to refer to them consciously as required. It should mean that when people deviate from values they expect others to encourage them back on track. They appreciate that guidance when they receive it.

Advertising slogans such as the one for Ford, *Quality Is Job 1*, and Lexus, *The Relentless Pursuit of Perfection*, can be value statements if used to guide behavior on all tasks. Ford would need a clearly shared understanding of what *quality* means and how that should guide every task and every decision about tasks. It should mean the following: no task continues if quality is being violated, everyone should be responsible for making sure quality is the first priority, adherence to quality standards is a major part of everyone's performance appraisal, and stories are circulated about people who withstood other demands, including cost and profit needs, if they had any negative effects on quality. Values such as those for Ford and Lexus pick up one of their major priorities and probably hint at the types of core competencies they would seek. It then can become part of the strategy of their suppliers to support those core values. To truly succeed, suppliers may need to operate with similar values of their own.

Laying the Groundwork (Perceiving)

Values drive behavior. Therefore, the first thing to do is to concentrate on existing and desired behavior in different parts of the business, such as meetings, customer relations, employee relations, and daily work activities. As you observe the behavior that currently exists, think about what people in the organization would say are the motives for the behavior. Also consider what people outside the organization who experience the behavior would say about motives for the behavior. What would customers say about your motives in relations with them? The important thing to note here is that stated values are not important if they are not driving action. Behavior reveals the values that are currently in operation. As there will be only a few values, motives provide the link between the actual values and a wide range of specific actions.

Seeing the Value (Understanding)

Consider how the current behaviors and motives help your organization and hurt it. If they ultimately harm your organization, it is reasonable to assume that the desired values are not the current values. For example, it is not hard to imagine behavior inconsistent with values of respect for individuals or innovation. In meetings people may frequently ignore and discount the ideas of others. If failures routinely cause problems for people, they will be less likely to take the risk of innovation. As you evaluate the contribution of current motives, you may find that there are preferable motives that would connect to behavior that would enhance the company's standing in the industry. From these motives it is possible to arrive at core values by asking, *why is that motive important?* If the first answer does not seem like a core value, ask more *why* questions until your responses have more of a feeling of being a core value.

Moving Forward (Reasoning)

Once you have core values identified from the processes above or simply look at ones the company already identified, evaluate how current processes, procedures, or systems support or contradict those core values. Think about how to reinforce the things that support core values and stop or alter the things that contradict core values. Recognize that core values are important to have only because there are numerous possibilities for situations to occur in which it would be expedient to ignore values. If these temptations did not arise, there would be no reason to identify core values. It is quite easy to claim the high ground when there is no difficulty. Core values are necessary as guiding lights in ambiguous situations. Therefore, consider the support given to people to stay on course with core values.

Vision and Goal Hierarchy

Although value statements may seem similar from one organization to another, vision statements should be distinctive. Many companies may have the same values of integrity in business relationships or supporting employee creativity, but a vision should sound specific to a business. The vision reflects the kind of future that it is trying to create. A vision is an image or picture of the future. The vision statement is the title of the picture to evoke a whole sense of it. A vision is an aspiration. Therefore, it should feel inspiring to the people of the organization. Visions need sufficient clarity that it is easy to grasp the feeling of living in that future. Microsoft's vision has these qualities—*A computer on every desk and in every home.*

Although it has this degree of clarity and focus, a vision is not about a particular point in time. It is paradoxical. It needs to be believable and possible, creating a plausible chance of organization success. At the same time it needs to be challenging and almost unreachable—*an impossible dream.* It is valuable for a vision to have this freeing, unrestricted feel to it.

The vision sits at the top of a pyramid. The remainder of the pyramid is the goal hierarchy. Through the goal hierarchy the organization is able to become significantly more specific and have measurable achievements for its success. It is a mistake to put the degree of specificity necessary for useful goals on a vision. Allow the vision to be an inspiring and powerful statement. Most important, the vision is not about the company. *We will be the leading supplier of wombat pacifiers and be on the vanguard of technology.* Statements such as this are thinly disguised goals about market share or technological accomplishments. The goals are fine; they are not statements of vision. A goal reflects desired business achievements; goals focus on the business. A vision reflects desired contributions by the business to the world around it; visions focus on the business' environment. You can successfully run a business with goals and no vision. On the other hand, regardless of how inspiring the vision, it is difficult to operate without goals. Therefore, if you are going to have a vision, use it to say something significant beyond your important business goals.

A vision statement should be as succinct as possible, certainly not longer than a sentence. Often, only a few words, where each word is like an image carrying much greater meaning, express the most valuable visions. You can use longer paragraphs to describe the meaning of key words within the statement of vision.

Laying the Groundwork (Perceiving)

In creating a vision it is useful to start with some image of a desired future. Scenario planning was different from this. In that case we were trying to determine how different environmental forces could converge in coherent and plausible ways. With vision we are choosing a future to inspire people in the company. There are several ways to get an image of worthwhile futures:

- Brainstorm wild dreams, unbridled speculations, and unbelievable possibilities for the future.
- Identify prophesies for the future—an optimistic view of environmental forces and shock waves.
- Discuss hopes for the future that make it substantially different from the present.
- Identify major changes in your industry you would like to see.

Seeing the Value (Understanding)

Combine the alternative futures from the previous phase of this process with your company's current and potential capability to identify aspirations the organization can pursue. As you choose a vision from this process, recognize that it must be personally inspiring. Otherwise, traditional business goals would be sufficient measures of achievement. Consider your commitment to any of the ideas, your determination to make that future real, the effort you are truly able to expend, and your willingness to work toward a vision that may be realized after your career with the organization.

Moving Forward (Reasoning)

Vision suggestions need to be specific and clear enough so that people can imagine themselves within the vision and can see real possibilities for efforts to attain it. Therefore, consider how the aspiration in this vision will influence behavior and performance within the organization. Identify issues that can arise to deflect people from the vision's direction as they do their work and determine how you will sustain a high level of energy and commitment to the vision within the organization.

Purpose

Purpose can be an answer to the question, *why is that vision important?* If your answer moves in the direction of benefits to the business, you are heading back to goals. The purpose of an organization cannot be profit any more than breathing is a purpose of life. Profit is, however, a significant goal. For example, if Microsoft said the purpose of their vision was to have expanded demand for software-related products, they would be talking about goals. When this happens, it is better to state the goal as a key business achievement; it is not a purpose.

Purpose statements may be simple or have several sentences, as you are describing the importance and significance of the vision and the organization. You are providing detailed responses to questions such as, *Why is the vision worthwhile? Why is this organization in existence? Why are we in business?* By answering either of the last two questions directly, it is possible to articulate a purpose without having a vision. Purpose helps make part of the vision a living reality even as work is being done to achieve that vision. Suppose Microsoft had responded that the purpose was to aid decision making, have information readily available whenever someone wanted it, or improve opportunities for learning and development. These kinds of statements say why the vision is important. As they implement their strategy they can be sure that they are on track toward their vision by making sure their efforts are in line with the purpose.

No matter how inspiring a vision may seem, it is still only a description of what the desired future is. It may be motivating but not provide sufficient guidance for the work used to achieve it. Purpose is the reason that future is valuable. We can adhere to the purpose in the present. If we think about the purpose as we work, we stand a much better chance of having our actions reflect our desire for the future. A vision is about a new future; it means a change from the present. Therefore, by responding to the importance of a vision, purpose picks up the benefits of that change to other players, especially customers. That is why we can focus on benefits, *why are we in business?*, without having a vision. With this benefit aspect of purpose we are returning, perhaps, to the strategic lever of delivering value. A purpose may work well for the business if it is doing nothing more than capturing in a clear, broad stroke the key value delivery choices of the business.

Laying the Groundwork (Perceiving)

Identify the major changes that your vision represents and consider how those changes affect customers and other players.

Seeing the Value (Understanding)

Focus on the benefits different groups would receive from those changes. Benefits include value delivered to a wider range of priorities, expanded opportunities, and reduced threats. Develop a purpose that will guide people in the company as they work toward the vision so that customers and other players can experience some of the benefits in the present, rather than only at some distant time in the future or once the company attains its vision. If you do not have a vision, you can identify similar types of benefits by using the question, *why are we in business?*

Moving Forward (Reasoning)

Consider the major initiatives or types of activities that you will need to achieve your goals or vision. Determine how you will use the purpose to provide explicit guidance as people are working on these initiatives. Purpose clearly is useful to guide the implementation of strategy. Values provide guidance to behavior by setting principled standards. Purpose provides guidance to behavior by directing it toward important accomplishments or contributions made by the business.

CHAPTER 24

Following One Path

Initial Thoughts

The essence of this process is pulling everything together into a single coherent direction for the future to advance the company's competitive advantage.

A strategy clearly describes how the company intends to achieve its main goals and move toward its vision. It describes the organization's main approach critical to creating the necessary value within the product or service, enabling the customer to experience that value, establishing the organization's market and industry distinctiveness, positioning itself to take advantage of windows of opportunity, and using its resources and capabilities to influence or respond to the evolving course of events in its industry so that it can continue to provide necessary customer benefits. It describes how the organization channels its strengths, protects its weaknesses, and uses its core competencies so that it can effectively position itself to deliver value, shift paradigms, or select critical success factors. It describes how the organization intends to face opportunities, threats, and constraints existing in the environment. It also describes how it intends to use and build core competencies to create company extensions and growth beyond the current market or industry. The strategy creates a strong sense of the immediate future; it makes the probable actions for achieving major corporate goals quite clear. At the same time it gives an indication of where the company is heading for the longer term.

A good strategy is not too general; banned words such as *best, high quality,* or *industry leader* do not permeate it. On the other hand, it is not so specific that it reduces room for flexibility or maneuverability. Strategy should be intelligible outside the business even if it is treated as confidential. It is telling the world how you intend to conduct business. It should be understandable to nearly anyone affected by the organization. It should contain specific ideas that the customer would value. It should challenge your competitors or create fear within them. It should also inspire employees to act.

A traditional mission statement can be the preamble to the strategy. It is more of a brief inspiring statement. If the banned words creep into the mission statement, be sure your strategy focuses on the true meaning. For example, if you must have a mission such as *continually crossing the boundary of technology to create high-quality products,* make sure the longer exposition of strategy addresses what these ideas mean in your business and how you are going to make it happen. If it implies core competencies, talk about them specifically. In any event, the strategy must explicitly link the mission statement to the vision and the detailed thinking you invested in understanding the environment, possible futures, and strategic levers. The strategy can start with a list of a few key items that make the mission statement more explicit. It becomes even more specific by continuing to ask, *how are we going to do that?* A strategy is not simply a sequence of moves, although it is better to err on the side of being too specific and action oriented. At some point the line starts to be crossed between strategy and the actions planned to implement the strategy. This is a gray area. Consider the strategy more of a description of the main areas in which actions occur and the coordination of those actions across the entire organization.

Laying the Groundwork (Perceiving)

Drop all peripheral ideas and get essential statements about your strategy. Create a mission statement if you feel there is value in having a simple, broad phrasing of what your company will do. Whether or not you want a mission statement as a preamble, you should articulate specific plans for *how* you will:

- Use strengths and core competencies to pursue your chosen opportunities for delivering value, shifting paradigms, or selecting critical success factors.
- Position the company to exploit windows of opportunity.
- Build strengths or reduce your weaknesses to deal with the threats you feel likely to occur and the constraints you are likely to meet.
- Establish the company's market and industry competitive distinctiveness.
- Channel company resources and capabilities to influence (or respond to) the evolving course of events within the industry and open new opportunities.
- Use core competencies to extend the company in new directions.
- Achieve major company goals.

Seeing the Value (Understanding)

You have now described a strategy. We are going to use core values, vision, and purpose to mold it. These ideas are useless without a clear connection to the strategy. People will notice the gap and the possibly resulting cynicism will reduce the level of effort for the strategy. Explicitly consider how the strategy reflects the core values. If it seems to contradict them, the strategy must change. Think about how you will use the core values as you implement the strategy. Be clear about how the strategy will lead to the future described in the vision. If the connection does not seem strong enough, change the strategy or modify the vision. Although the vision is an aspiration for the future, it also needs to be realistic. The strategy reveals its realism by being the best path to it. Finally, the benefits articulated in the purpose must provide focused guidance for the strategy. Think about how the strategy will begin creating these benefits as you implement it. After you fine-tune the strategy, it, in combination with the core values, vision, purpose, and mission, should form a coherent description of the company.

Moving Forward (Reasoning)

With the strategy so carefully created and modified, we should be finished. We're close. In this phase of the process I want to address three distinct but related issues to shape the strategy and be sure it covers what is really necessary: multitiered industry definitions, industry life cycle, and the scope of mission. Each of these issues has interesting implications for strategy. We'll look at them in order.

Multitiered Industries

When we created the business field map in Chapter 11 we were trying to avoid some of the pitfalls of the typical narrow industry definitions that overly restrict one's view of the real forces at play. The field contained a significantly more expanded view. We looked at multitiered industries. For example, what is the proper industry label for a fast food chain? The answer is that, similar to any business, it operates in several industries. It is useful to see one's company enmeshed in a variety of industries ranging from very narrow definitions to rather broad ones. As part of the fast food industry it pays attention to menu selection and marketing techniques of its obvious direct competitors—the other fast food chains. As part of the restaurant industry it may look at trends in meals eaten away from the home, patterns of eating to determine the best locations, and competitors for the food dollar who offer a more full-service approach at reasonable prices. As part of the food services industry it may consider changing technology in food preparation and storage, sources of food supplies, and food regulation. Maybe it is also part of the travel industry or the out-of-home family entertainment industry. The clear fact is that each industry definition provides insight into the business that it would miss if it chose only one way to look at itself. A narrow definition is certainly myopic and limited as it misses some of the major forces and players surrounding the business. A broad definition, on the other hand, neglects some of the important details to make a strategy successful. Check your strategy with a variety of industry definitions to determine how you are effectively addressing the different issues that arise as you alter your view of your industry.

Industry Life Cycle

Industry life cycle is a simple play on the traditional product life cycle view. Some people seem to think that rapid technological change has shortened product life so much that it is a useless concept. Regardless of the length of the cycle, however—a few weeks to several years—it is still a fairly accurate image of product stages. In addition, many technological changes may make things smaller or faster but the basic product remains the same. For strategic purposes it is more useful to think on the industry level. For example, in the personal computer industry there is fairly rapid technological advance. A purchase is practically outdated as soon as it's removed from the box. It would seem then that the products have a short life cycle. The industry's life cycle, however, is more interesting. Where would you place it in these seven typical stages of the cycle, which can be compared to the seven ages described in William Shakespeare's *As You Like It?*

> All the world's a stage
> And all the men and women merely players:
> They have their exits and their entrances;
> And one man in his time plays many parts,
> His acts being seven ages.

Development—Birth of the industry.

> At first the infant,
> Mewing and puking in the nurse's arms.

Growth—The rate of sales growth is highest.

> Then the whining school boy, with his satchel
> And shining morning face, creeping like snail
> Unwilling to school.

Shakeout—Growth rate slows and some firms fall under competitive pressure.

> And then the lover,
> Sighing like a furnace, with a woeful ballad
> Made to his mistress' eyebrow.

Maturity—Minor growth but there are plenty of profitable opportunities, so firms battle over share of a relatively stable customer base and new firms may be attracted to enter.

> Then a soldier,
> Full of strange oaths, and bearded like the pard,
> Jealous in honor, sudden and quick in quarrel,
> Seeking the bubble reputation
> Even in the cannon's mouth.

Saturation—Growth and sales come from only demographic changes. Companies are well established.

> And then the justice,
> In fair round belly with good capon lined,
> With eyes severe and beard of formal cut,
> Full of wise saws and modern instances;
> And so he plays his part.

Decline—Demand drops off. Cost control is critical. There are no real attempts to make changes.

> The sixth age shifts
> Into the lean and slippered pantaloon,
> With spectacles on nose and pouch on side,
> His youthful hose, well saved, a world too wide
> For his shrunk shank; and his manly voice,
> Turning again toward childish treble, pipes
> And whistles in his sound.

Extinction—Some sales still remain. Most companies have left the industry.

> Last scene of all,
> That ends this strange eventful history,
> Is second childishness and mere oblivion,
> Sans teeth, sans eyes, sans taste, sans everything.
>
> WILLIAM SHAKESPEARE, *As You Like It*

Despite the rapidly changing product technology that renders one generation of products after another obsolete, the personal computer industry seems to be in the shakeout or maturity stage. Strategy certainly varies depending upon the stage of an industry's life cycle. I do not mean to complicate matters, but it is a good idea to assess each of the stages in the multitiered view. Perhaps with the personal computer industry, one would experiment with other industry definitions such as computers, information processing, and home entertainment. It is necessary to make sure the chosen strategy is consistent with the relevant stage for each industry definition.

Consider some of the typical strategic influences in the first four stages. In the development stage, no company has any advantage other than what its core competencies create. There are great uncertainties, possibilities, and hazards. Customers are unsure of the value and whether the industry will satisfy existing priorities. The customers are risk takers as they, along with the companies in the industry, may be searching for new priorities. There are no paradigms in place.

In the growth stage customers certainly see the value; each company works hard to cause value delivery to move in its favor. They are selecting different critical success factors as there are no proven paths to success. The interesting paradox is that the growth is accelerated by more companies participating. It is difficult for a single company to grow the market. It is better to have a market share of a rapidly expanding pie than 100 percent of a pie that never grows. It is important to keep an eye on the long view, or the dynamic nature of the short run may cause a company to be on the losing end in the next stage. The profit levels and potential are attractive to many companies and the number of players expands greatly from the development stage. Companies may enter the industry who have well-developed strengths and core competencies.

In the shakeout stage some critical success factors have prevailed while others have proved irrelevant. Companies begin duplicating each other in order to stay in contention. There is a heavier pressure to find something that is distinctive. Core competencies are better established from experience in the industry. Customers also have more experience with the industry. Therefore, they have a greater ability to articulate their priorities and choose among the competing companies. Competitive advantage may be gained from how well the company manages its own operation or its relations with other players in the industry.

In the maturity stage paradigms have become more firmly embedded within the industry. Successful companies have well-established core competencies and frequently a loyal company base. It is difficult to build market share dramatically. Strategies will be focused on critical success factors regarding production or organization if the company has better profit potential from controlling internal operations. Many industries remain relatively mature for a period of many years, but new product innovations that create or meet emerging customer priorities can alter the competitive landscape. For example, the automobile industry is a long-term, highly competitive, mature industry. New players do manage to enter but they invariably must win market share from existing competitors. They usually do this by further segmenting the market and targeting niches with specific priorities. Mature industries, given their established nature, are more vulnerable to having the rules changed by newer or more aggressive competitors. An aggressive company doing this must have the core competency necessary for the new paradigm they are trying to introduce.

Scope of Mission

Whether or not there is a formal mission statement, there is still some range or scope to the entire strategic effort. The last of these three issues to shape the strategy and test its value is to look at what the company is attempting to accomplish. Strategies can fall into a few general categories:

- Value delivery modifications.
- Industry evolution.
- Crossing industry boundaries.
- Building new industries.

These categories define points on a continuum; there are clear differences among the categories with plenty of gray areas in between. As we talk about these four categories, the overlap with multitiered industry definitions and industry life cycles will be apparent. The first category—value delivery modifications—includes strategies to improve, refine, or excel with products that remain relatively unchanged. It is possible to alter product features to tap different priorities. There are no shifting paradigms but there may be attempts to better align with existing customer paradigms or leverage the deeply held ones that will not shift. Core competencies will not be changing much but companies will always be looking for ways to improve the competencies they do possess. The environment seems relatively stable in that scenarios or shock waves with dramatic shifts in the industry seem highly unlikely. This category for mission scope is very typical for industries in the shakeout through saturation stages. The main competitive arena for strategy may be a focus on particular critical success factors. For example, companies will focus on brand names if the value of the product does not justify a search by customers for product information—they are willing to rely upon reputation. Companies will focus on breadth of product line if customers are likely to trade up to higher priced items as their incomes increase or adjust their purchases as personal situations change, as they do for insurance and other financial services as they age.

When the scope of the mission centers on industry evolution, more things are put into play. This often happens when there are major changes in the environment. For example, a removal or reduction of government regulation initiates a rapid industry evolution. Consider the airline and telecommunication industries. Well-run, highly profitable companies have seen their fortunes improve or their positions erode as they had to deal with the new realities of the industry. Paradigms shift, the old rules of success do not work. The industry's evolution becomes an opportunity to some and a threat to others. It is necessary to shift the scope of mission from the value delivery category that succeeded in the regulatory era to the industry evolution category. Similarly, industry evolution occurs due to major technological changes. For example, in the personal computer industry, as long as the change is confined to things such as faster processing speeds and more storage, we are probably looking at strategies in the value delivery category. The scope of the mission may shift to the industry evolution category when there is highly refined voice recognition software or high-resolution flat screens. Strategy must include focusing core competencies on new paradigms or critical success factors. It is frequently industry evolution that pumps new life into mature industries and may put them back into a high growth stage. The competitive landscape is more lively with industry evolution, so it is important to have the strategy address potentially emerging competitors who may be crossing over from other industries.

Businesses often try to influence an industry evolution when they decide to merge with or acquire other players—suppliers, distributors, providers of complementary products, or strategic partners. For example, although it was short-lived, a few years ago United Airlines became Allegis—a travel company with rental cars, hotels, and airplanes. This seemed a logical move for a company in the travel industry; many customers use all three services when they travel. It may have failed because it was a broad industry definition. The scope of the mission was crossing industry boundaries from the airline industry to the rental car and hotel industry. If each industry requires a different core competency, the merger cannot work easily. A company successfully crosses industry boundaries only when it has a core competency that is relevant to other industries. Therefore, this third category for mission scope is heavily dependent upon having a well-developed core competency that can be competitively applied in another industry. This airline example also points out the need to sustain a multitiered industry view.

When the scope of the mission is building a new industry, we are in the development stage of the life cycle and, therefore, we need to build core competencies. No company will have enough experience to have the necessary range of core competencies. For example, when the personal computer industry began to grow we saw DEC decline significantly and IBM stumble severely. Although they were in the computer industry, it is likely that the strong core competencies they had for the mainframe computer industry were not easily transferred. They needed to build new core competencies for the new industry. They were certainly in position to develop these, but their strategies failed to accommodate this need.

CHAPTER 25

Maneuvering Through Shifting Terrain

Initial Thoughts

The essence of this process is preparing for the inevitable changes that will greet the carefully chosen strategy.

As they say, *the best laid plans of mice and men often go astray*. We chose a path to follow for a strategy. There is no reason to expect that path to remain exactly as we expected. When we designed the strategy we tried to see it in dynamic terms as things would be changing. We typically ignore, however, the effects of our own actions on that environment. It is like playing chess and assuming that every move will happen as planned. We know that the opponent will move in response to us. Chess is the anticipation of a series of moves and countermoves. Similarly, in strategy we must expect that competitors and other players will react to our strategy. For example, a strategy in a mature industry usually targets increased market share at the expense of competitors; it would be reasonable to expect them to respond. Amateurs may make mistakes, but it is preferable to think like a chess master playing another master. It could be costly to have a strategy depend upon the ignorance of a competitor even if the strategy takes advantage of paradigms that restrict their thinking. Maybe they will be slow, but they will respond when sales decline. We want to anticipate the dynamic nature of the competitive field as the company and its competitors pursue visions, actualize strategies, and react to each other.

The second reason for maneuvering on the strategic path is the revelation of the accuracy of assumptions as the future starts happening. We never know the future with certainty, so we use assumptions to move past this and make decisions. The most likely scenario represents our more confident assumptions. Whether or not we expect shock waves to occur reflects more assumptions. The whole trail of the strategic thinking cycle is littered with assumptions. We will find out soon enough if our assumptions about the future were on target. By the law of averages some of the assumptions will miss their mark. The decision may need adjustment to accommodate the reality that does unfold. In addition, the world overflows with complex information; it is neither possible nor desirable to obtain and process all of it. There is some information we can never obtain; for example, we can guess at the thinking of our competitors but we can never fully know it. Therefore, uncertainty and ambiguity are eternal features of strategy.

A tolerance, even enjoyment, of ambiguity is a major capability of a good strategic thinker who does not rush to some quick conclusions because things are unsettled or difficult to understand. There is patience for pursuing additional knowledge but this is not an endless process. It is tempered by an ability to assess the potential value of new information and a willingness to make assumptions. We spoke about these issues in Chapter 5. Any company will have significant information about the entire strategic environment. The only way to move from the information or knowledge base to a strategic decision is through assumptions. Assumptions about the future are necessary to make strategic decisions. If we did not make assumptions, our uncertainty about the future would freeze us into indecisiveness and inaction. On the other hand, assumptions do not remove uncertainty. It is, to some extent, an attempt at an intelligent prediction, but the future could unfold in a completely different manner.

It is important to be absolutely explicit about assumptions to avoid the trap that happens so frequently in people's thinking—they forget that they made assumptions to arrive at their decisions and begin to believe they are operating by unalterable truths. Assumptions are the basis of paradigms. Paradigms, if unexamined, create rigid thinking and block people from seeing changes that may be occurring. As the future changes we start to find that competitors, unencumbered by our assumptions and paradigms, are able to create more effective market strategies. As we go through this thinking process we will look at both competitive dynamics and responsiveness to assumptions. This is a process of anticipation—*what if x happens, how would we respond?*

Laying the Groundwork (Perceiving)

Competitive Dynamics

The first step is an important one: an assessment of the relative capabilities—strengths, weaknesses, and core competencies—of competitors. It is important in this assessment to look at current and potential competitors as you move through the multitiered industry definition. Each industry definition gives a different view of the business field map. It is important to look at narrow definitions as well as broad definitions. The relative assessment compares capabilities of competitors with each other and your company with respect to the general market environment—trends in forces, patterns, scenarios, and potential shock waves. It also matches capabilities with opportunities, threats, and constraints in delivering value, shifting paradigms, and selecting critical success factors. You would also want to determine the ability of competitors to influence industry evolution, cross industry boundaries, or create new industries.

Responsiveness to Assumptions

If you look back at the major strategic thinking cycle, you will notice numerous occasions when an assumption was necessary to continue thinking. As you were moving among the different processes trying to advance your conclusions in each, it was never possible to operate with complete knowledge about any environmental component. It is extremely useful to have a net to catch the assumptions as thinking progresses. You want to have an assumption list, no matter how extensive. There will be many assumptions. Every environmental force requires an assumption. The way you handled shock waves and different scenarios implies additional assumptions. If you had a natural temptation to develop best and worst case scenarios in contrast to your most likely case, you can see that these scenarios occur by varying assumptions about environmental, market, or business conditions, from being extremely favorable to being extremely unfavorable. Your thinking may benefit by returning to your work on scenarios to create ones that are truly distinctive from each other, emphasizing different conditions as the core of the scenario, rather than variations on the same theme. These variations are easily handled in the work you do in the thinking process of this chapter.

You want to be clear about how you used assumptions to draw conclusions in strategic thinking—how much did decisions depend upon the assumption? Assumptions do not reduce uncertainty; they are our mechanism for facing it. Therefore, they need to be realistic and logically consistent—a defensible judgment based on the information and knowledge you possess. Assumptions should not be a substitute for obtainable information. Most important, avoid assumptions made for convenience or to fit your strategic ideas. *We want to do the following. If only the world looks like x in the future, then we will be successful. Therefore, we assume that the world will be x.* Nobody will be that misguided in making assumptions, but it is easy to see how passion about a strategy can lead to healthy optimism about the future and influence assumptions. It is preferable to derive assumptions by looking at the uncertainty you have about the environment rather than the desire you have for a particular decision. You can try to design a strategy that begins to mold the world to your vision. You want to look at the assumptions, however, with clear, objective eyes so you can have a strategy that meets the conditions you are likely to face.

Seeing the Value (Understanding)

Competitive Dynamics

My computer cheats when it plays chess. The authorities would banish me if I sat with another person and looked in an encyclopedia of moves and counter-moves each time it was my turn. The computer must be immune from prosecution; it is the encyclopedia. It looks at a possible move, considers my counter-moves, then its response to my countermoves, then my response and so on. It tracks multiple paths and then makes a choice. I have only one tactic to give me a chance to win—choose the *move now* command and cause it to choose before it can test the alternatives. The computer's relatively impulsive move puts it on my level of play.

Unfortunately, to some extent we need to be the unrestricted computer in regard to our strategy. There is an industry dynamic in which moves by your company, competitors, customers, and other environment players continually shift the opportunities, threats, and constraints presented to each other. Your strategy is an initiative in the industry that alters the terrain for other players; they will respond. Use your knowledge of relative strengths, weaknesses, and core competencies from the previous phase of this thinking process. *How are different competitors likely to respond once you implement your strategy? How would you then react? How are different players likely to respond? Do they accelerate the likelihood of your strategy's success by taking supportive actions or do they create threats or constraints? Your strategy must deliver benefits to your customers. Do they take actions, other than buying your product or service, that help your company? How do you respond?* It is a challenge with worthwhile results to think about alternative series of moves and countermoves. You can prepare your company to modify the strategy as its implementation creates a new terrain for others.

Responsiveness to Assumptions

As the future will not be entirely as expected, it is necessary to do a careful risk assessment of the effects of errors in assumptions. Classify your major assumptions using the degree of uncertainty you have about the assumption and the potential impact on your organization if the assumption is incorrect. Perhaps the two-by-two matrix in Figure 25–1—high and low impact versus high and low uncertainty—is a little simplistic, but it is a useful first-cut sorting mechanism. Choose a finer gradation for both dimensions if you have many assumptions to sort and want clearer distinctions among them. High uncertainty occurs when you have little information or questionable information and believe there is a high chance you will be wrong. Low uncertainty occurs when you are very confident of your information or knowledge. A high impact occurs when your strategy is highly dependent upon your assumption; if it proves incorrect you will need major alterations of the strategy, perhaps to the point of abandoning it. A low impact occurs when the assumption matters to the strategy but would require only minor modifications were it to be wrong. Clearly, you would want to look

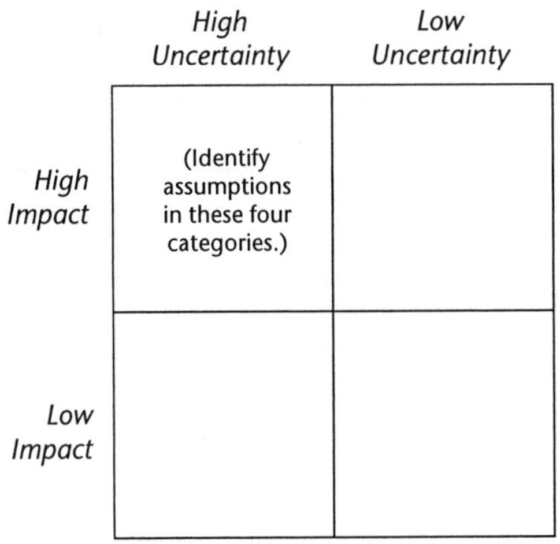

	High Uncertainty	Low Uncertainty
High Impact	(Identify assumptions in these four categories.)	
Low Impact		

Figure 25–1   High and Low Impact versus High and Low Uncertainty

at the high-risk, high-impact assumptions first. Get specific about the source of your uncertainty—*what precisely is leading you to a lower level of confidence in your assumption?* You also want to be specific about the kind of impact an error in the assumption has on your company and its strategy. *Will you need to make dramatic shifts in the strategy? Will your strengths or core competencies be sufficient? Will weaknesses create greater hazards?*

Moving Forward (Reasoning)

We always talk about being reactive—acting after the fact—as an undesirable state. Everyone wants to be proactive—acting before the fact. I would say we want our thinking to be proactive in that we anticipate problems before they happen. We probably want our strategy to be proactive—it reveals our intention to create something. Many of our actions, however, need to be reactive—we respond to something. What we want to do is get an early warning system in place so that we react before it escalates into an insurmountable hazard. We should eliminate this unnecessary concern between being reactive or proactive. Our thinking should prepare us to respond quickly to signs—observable facts or information—that alert us about a significant move by another player or an environmental shift that will render an assumption incorrect. Our intention should be a continual shrinking of response time until we anticipate events with enough time to act. We want to consciously address the factors that delay response time and change them.

The main chances we have to alter course are key events—major points in time when the company makes substantial commitments, enters new markets, accelerates the level of investment, and so forth. An important reason for identifying key events is that they are times when a shift in strategy will need to happen if the assumptions are proving incorrect or there are any unanticipated, negative or positive, changes in the environment of the company. Key events are times for:

- Countermoves to the actions of other players.
- The greatest possibilities and hazards.
- The full force of the risk in assumptions or moves by players to affect the ultimate success of the organization.
- The company to contract or expand dramatically.
- The company to bail out completely from the chosen path.

Therefore, we want the early warning system to signal upcoming change with enough time to react prior to a key event. We need an information tracking system to keep the company current with its environment. We want trigger points in the information—clearly identified data that we believe foretell an assumption being proved incorrect, a move by a player, or the coming of a shock wave. When we discussed shock waves in Chapter 16 we noted the need for several decisions regarding:

- Methods to track information that would help anticipate the arrival of the shock wave.
- Triggers that would serve as warning signals to detect the shock wave in its early stages.
- Resources the company is willing to dedicate to maintain a state of preparedness for the potential arrival of a shock wave.

We need the same decisions to plan our countermoves and maintain strategic flexibility for assumptions. In addition, we want to go one step further and have some contingency plans—what we will do if a trigger alerts us to an upcoming change. Contingency plans are responses to the issues raised about competitive dynamics, assumptions, and shock waves. They describe initial ideas on possible changes in strategic decisions. Contingency plans can be fully formed alternative strategies; this would require considerable effort. This whole strategic thinking process represents a reasonable time commitment to explore fully the necessary issues to arrive at a strategic decision. When we say strategy is an ongoing process rather than an annual planning event, we are referring to this need to continually track unfolding events and maneuver the strategy through the turmoil. Therefore, contingency planning, even to the extent of a major change in the strategy, must be ongoing. It is costly to gather and track information. It is costly to devote personnel time to an ongoing strategic thinking effort. It is costly to dedicate resources for a state of readiness to alter course. All these costs are worthwhile if they are lower than the costs of delayed reactions. Ultimately, this decision on maneuvering in the shifting terrain we encounter in implementing a strategy hinges on a comparison of the costs of early reaction versus late reaction. We need to be careful because it is easier to see the short-term costs associated with preparing for an early reaction: a well-functioning information system, personnel time, and resource preparedness. It is harder to see the longer term costs associated with having a late reaction: missed opportunities, expanded threats, or towering constraints.

Let's be realistic. You do not want detailed contingency plans. When the time comes to change or modify your strategic direction you are not going to search through the office file cabinets to implement what you decided in the past. You will need to respond to the conditions as you face them. Contingency planning has a different value. You may gain some insight about conditions into the future that you want to include in the initial strategy. Furthermore, by thinking ahead you can build the capability to remain alert and respond. They are mental contingencies—getting the mind into position to shrink response time. Or, if you insist, become more proactive.

Making the Strategy Work

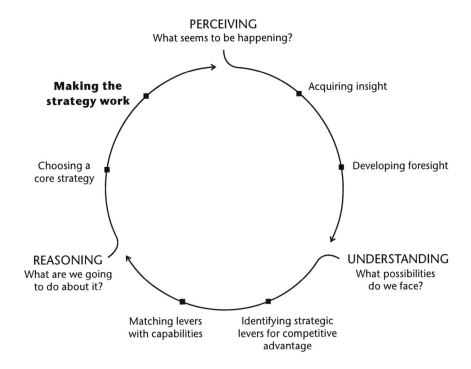

PERCEIVING
What seems to be happening?

Making the
strategy work

Acquiring insight

Choosing a
core strategy

Developing foresight

REASONING
What are we going
to do about it?

UNDERSTANDING
What possibilities
do we face?

Matching levers
with capabilities

Identifying strategic
levers for competitive
advantage

CHAPTER 26

Setting Goals

Initial Thoughts

The essence of this process is identifying a connected series of goals to drive the strategy and the actions to make it work.

Figure 23–1 showed the relationship of the goal hierarchy to vision, values, purpose, and mission. In this chapter we want to explore the goal hierarchy a little further and in relation to the actions needed to make the strategy work. We will discuss the areas for actions in the next chapter. A goal hierarchy, shown in Figure 26–1, is analogous to a pyramid going from the most sweeping (covering the whole organization) and longest term goals near the top through layers of division goals and task force goals to the most detailed at the bottom—specific, short-term goals for different tasks. Therefore, a goal hierarchy has two major aspects: a time sequencing of goals and the range of activities relevant to different goals. Usually we accomplish things from the bottom up. Achieving goals at the bottom of the pyramid leads to achieving goals at higher levels. Therefore, a time sequence is analogous to building the pyramid from the bottom to its apex. Goals at the bottom cover fewer activities; goals at higher levels cover increasingly larger numbers of activities.

Goals at all levels in the hierarchy need to be:

- Written—to clarify necessary commitments.
- Understandable—to create a concrete picture in the mind.
- Challenging—to generate a sense of energy.
- Measurable—to convey a specific target for accomplishment.

- Time oriented—to create the appropriate level of stress through the pressure of deadlines.
- Achievable—to give a reasonable chance of success.

The goal hierarchy allows the kind of freedom one needs to have a broad, sweeping, inspiring vision. The vision must exhibit the company's commitment to a future in the environment. If the vision starts to address the company's position in the industry, its technological prowess, or its products, then it is more appropriate to label the ideas as goals and drop the vision statement. Most so-called visions that we see in companies are goal statements. There is a difference between the type of thinking we do for vision and the type we do for goals. Vision thinking is about the external environment. The goals, even at the top, usually focus on achievements that benefit the company.

The level of the pyramid below the vision contains the main corporate goals. These are traditional business goals such as profit levels, market share, market growth rates, and technological leadership. These significant goals require contributions by all parts of the company. It is easy to see the sequence of movement through the hierarchy: as individuals achieve their goals they enable work

Figure 26–1   The Goal Hierarchy

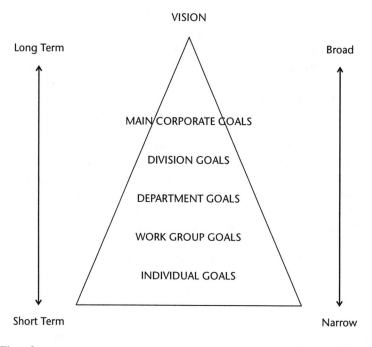

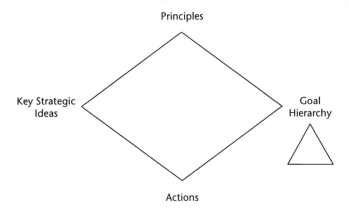

Figure 26–2   Implementing Strategy

groups to achieve goals, which in turn lead to the department, division, and main corporate goals. The relationship between main corporate goals and the vision is not as obvious. Achieving all corporate goals does not ensure attainment of the vision. The vision and goals serve two separate but related purposes for the strategy. The vision keeps the company focused on its environment, the main goals on its own success. The strategy must lead to both. The hierarchy's sequence from bottom to top shows why it is easy to have vision lost in the shuffle. It requires extra effort to keep the vision in people's awareness as the daily pressures are going to move people's efforts in the flow of work-related goals.

The strategy targets the main corporate goals and the vision. Goals lower in the pyramid are milestones along the road and therefore are more directly connected to actions used to implement the strategy. It is perhaps a little easier to see these connections as represented in Figure 26–2.

The relationship among these four elements is quite simple. The goals in the hierarchy capture the desired achievements. The key strategic ideas are specific elements from the strategy. Actions are the specific activities in a variety of areas, discussed in the next chapter, to make those ideas work and meet the goals. One way to make core values important in an organization is to think of different major arenas for action and create principles to guide behavior for those actions.

For example, suppose there is a main corporate goal of technological leadership. The strategy to achieve that would probably include building technical core competence through specific personnel skills and a level of investment in R&D activities. Actions to implement that strategy could involve hiring policies, training activities, collaborative work efforts, the structure of R&D processes, and the connection of R&D to operations and marketing activities. If the company had a core value of integrity it could derive specific principles to guide the different actions.

The connection among the four elements could also begin with strategy. Suppose the company had a strategy to create a broad product line to capture customers entering a market on the lower price end who may then trade up as their incomes increase. This is a major strategic element for a variety of companies, such as manufacturers of motorcycles, automobiles, and consumer electronics. That strategy could have market share goals for different products or target markets. Actions to implement the strategy and reach the goals could include product development and promotional activities. If the company had a core value of innovativeness, it could derive specific principles to guide its R&D activities.

CHAPTER 27

Taking Action

Initial Thoughts

The essence of this process is identifying the major actions needed throughout the organization to make the strategy succeed, achieve the goals, and eventually reach the vision.

It seems as if it's getting quite lonely and quiet here. Maybe it's just you and me left. The others experienced the excitement in creating a strategy, but now we face the hard work of making it happen. On the other hand, they may have been so energized that they ran to implement their ideas and reap the rewards. We are crossing the frontier from strategic planning to operational planning, shifting from thought to action, from reading to doing. To paraphrase Humphrey Bogart in *Casablanca*, "Where you're going, I can't follow." Therefore, I just want to make a few brief points about things to consider in key action arenas. Then, after some concluding remarks in the epilogue, I am also going to leave.

Key strategic actions describe what you need to do, how you are going to do it, who will be responsible, when it will occur (the timing or time frame), where it will occur (if that is relevant), and the resources needed to carry out that action effectively. They reveal the details of your organization's strengths and weaknesses. They demonstrate how the company uses its core competencies. They show how you are carrying out your strategy, using strategic levers, and maneuvering through the shifting terrain. As shown in Figure 26–2, the actions are guided by principles based on core values, aimed at achieving specific goals, and designed from key ideas in the strategy. In this chapter we will survey types of actions in a variety of areas pertinent to the strategy. Within each of these areas it will be necessary for you to do action planning: choosing the necessary actions, creating time schedules, assigning personnel responsibilities, and maintaining the connections with the remainder of the items on Figure 26–2—key strategic ideas, principles, and goals.

Serving the Customer

It is inevitable that a major part of the strategy will focus on value delivery to satisfy customer priorities. The traditional *four P's* of marketing—product, price, promotion, and place—provide a good starting point for some of the necessary actions for that part of strategy. We need a more expansive version of the basic marketing framework to be consistent with a full strategic, systems view of a dynamic market changing as the future unfolds. Thinking from the customers' perspective, we realize that the focus is not on products or service but a full value package. If not, there would only be one type of car, one kind of computer, and so forth. The fact that customers have such different experiences from each other with the same product leads to significant differences in product qualities to create different value experiences for different market segments. Product use is the major basis for assessing customer priorities. Actions in this area covers product design so the customer can extract the desired value from the product. Pre- and postsales services are other areas in which to plan actions that help the customers satisfy their priorities.

For example, an article in the July 13, 1996 issue of *The Economist* discussed how "a company will prosper if it marshals all its resources to solving a problem for a well-defined customer group." They gave an example of a German company that transformed itself from being a commercial dishwasher manufacturer into one concerned with problems of the target market segment—preventing water drops on glasses—rather than one concerned with advanced electronics which the customers did not know how to use. The article cited two books—*Simplicity Wins* by Gunter Rommel and *Hidden Champions* by Hermann Simon—that surveyed several midsized companies and found that success depended on focus for value delivery to satisfy customer priorities by having a narrower range of products and selling to fewer customers, or dominating market share of a narrow market to concentrate on design, quality, and service.

Actions to set prices require understanding of the industry's pricing structure, competitor pricing strategies, your own cost structure, and the relative competitiveness of your product. From the customer's perspective, however, the total transaction is not limited to the amount paid for your product. As a simple matter, we all know that credit terms affect many purchase decisions. For example, some people do not think that much about the total price of an automobile, only their monthly payments. Taking a larger view, it is important to consider all the transactions encountered by the customer prior to purchase, during purchase, and after purchase to use and service the product effectively. All these activities can involve the expenditure of funds in addition to the purchase price. To the extent that there are needs for complementary products or services, this will also enter the customer's thinking regarding economic transactions.

In addition, you should think about other transactions the customer must undertake to buy and use your product. Resource transactions are other commitments the customer must make to use your product. For example, in purchasing an appliance, you need to devote space to it. In running a supermarket, it is not possible to purchase every single product as there is a limited resource—shelf space. Psychological transactions include all of the mental and emotional experiences tied to the product and its use. Think of the way fear or insecurity enters insurance purchases. These types of transactions are critical to understanding the customer's perspective. You can consider actions related to the entire set of transactions encountered by customers in different market segments to do business with you and fully extract the value they seek from the product.

This difference between product price and full cost to the customer can be quite dramatic. A January 18, 1997 article in *The Economist* illuminated this difference for the looming battle between network PCs and stand-alone PCs. Although network PCs are less expensive to buy—$500 versus $1000–$1500—they may lose their advantage when the true, full costs to the customer are considered. The Gardner Group estimates that the lifetime cost of ownership to a company for a stand-alone PC can be more that $13,000 per year when you include maintenance, training, administration, technical support, and time lost by users fooling around with games and other diversions that make life worth living. The network PCs would require extra cost in the network and servers and may not save much on the other costs.

Traditional action areas relate to sales force, advertising, and other promotions to get the customer to buy the product. From this perspective one would also consider the way in which items such as packaging, brands, trademarks, reputation, or layout of facilities provide information to the customer. This is certainly important but not sufficient for a full strategic perspective. We need to consider promotion from the perspective of customer purchase behavior. They undergo a three-stage cycle prior to buying the product:

- Awareness of the product.
- Evaluation of the information they have received (or some other means of testing the product or the validity of the information).
- Seeking new information (either from you, your competitors, others in the industry, or product evaluation organizations).

In an expanded view, promotion is part of a larger information exchange with the customer. The cycle above is part of the presales information need. Customers need information during and after the sale. Consider actions to provide the whole range of information needed by customers to extract the value they seek from the product.

Place typically focuses upon distribution channels—methods to ensure access or availability of the product. It is a subtle but important shift in thinking from planning actions that gets the product flowing into channels to the customer's perspective of easy access or ready availability. In the traditional perspective, actions may focus on order taking and managing accounts receivable with distributors. From the latter perspective it is necessary to think about actions that make distributors considerably more effective in their efforts.

Managing Key Operational Processes

Operational processes—purchasing, production, inventory control, and delivery—typically support the strategic actions chosen for serving the customer. For example, in looking at *place* we considered easy access to the product by the customer. This is frequently an issue of time to the customer—how rapidly they can get the product or service. Therefore, managing the workflow is important. Workflow is an all-encompassing term indicating all operational processes. This immediately raises strategic issues for the company—taking the necessary actions to identify and manage key processes that support the value you are trying to create and deliver to customers in the cost and time frame established when you thought about serving the customer. Workflow is also the main focal point for quality control efforts.

It is possible to compete by increasing efficiency and lowering costs by reducing the time needed to complete the workflow cycle, reducing the material and personnel requirements for the workflow, or improving product quality. It is important to focus on significant aspects of the workflow cycles that allow for competitive advantage. The strategic significance of reengineering can be seen in this focus on workflow processes. Michael Hammer and James Champy (*Reengineering the Corporation*) laid the important groundwork for this effort. In Michael Hammer's latest book (*Beyond Reengineering*) he intensifies the focus on key operational processes by calling for the entire structuring of the organization around those key processes and defining jobs in relation to process contributions. It may be useful to follow his specific advice, but the more important point is to sustain the focus on the strategic significance of managing key operational processes.

Actions to manage key operational processes provides the groundwork for several strategic issues you need to consider: technological changes leading to process innovation, the competitive dynamics of maintaining a cost advantage in industry, the potential for increasing quality, the flexibility of facilities for adapting the workflow cycles to meet multiple uses or necessary changes, the level of capacity utilization you will experience at different stages of market growth, the possibility of increasing capacity to meet growing market demands, the degree of automation/computerization, the skill requirements for people, and the impact of organizational forms (e.g., teams) on workflow effectiveness and efficiency.

Pursuing Ongoing Innovation

Research and development are critical strategic issues in two important areas:

- Product or customer value package—the evolution of the product over time and innovation of new products.
- Technological change and innovation in key operational processes—the creation of the product.

The need for action planning is quite simple—things change. You can either lead your industry, follow the leader, or fall behind. The odds of simply staying in the same position and never changing are extremely small. You must give consideration to innovation efforts needed to remain competitive. Consider previous innovations of the product by yourself and others. Use your earlier thinking about the technological forces in the environment as they relate to the technological evolution of your operation processes, products, and industry. Your action planning should clearly reflect the means by which you will address strategic initiatives related to innovation and improvement.

Organizing for Success

A new vision represents a change to the organization. A new strategy plots a course into the future that diverges from the status quo. It would be remarkably fortuitous if the existing organizational structure, management methods, and other human resource processes perfectly matched the new direction. Change will be necessary in the way people organize to work together. There have been many books on forward-looking leadership, including my own, *From Sage to Artisan: The Nine Roles of the Value Driven Leader*. My purpose is different from these approaches to leadership. Rather than advocating a particular style of leadership or organization, I want to look at these issues in a strategic sense and promote an important focus. People drive the strategy through the actions they take in serving the customer, managing key operational processes, and pursuing ongoing innovation. Therefore, leadership, organization design, and the handling of any personnel issue must support the strategy of the organization.

There is one other strategically related driving force in organizing for success. We spoke about a variety of opportunities, threats, and constraints, but the organization can have self-imposed constraints when it does not fully use its capabilities or potential. The reason is that during turbulent times we often want to exercise more control and seek that through more rules and structure. On the other hand, we praise smaller firms because they often have less time to create an organization structure and operate with flexibility that gives individuals greater latitude in their work. Flexibility is inevitably necessary in a company that values strategic thinking and recognizes that a move into the future is not cast in concrete. Too many rules creates a lethargic organization with little thinking and less chance for strategic success.

Regardless of your strategy and your industry-related core competencies, I have been claiming that thinking is a core competency relevant to any organization. It is the heart of any learning organization and the foundation of building knowledge as a significant corporate asset. The chapters in the early part of this book addressed important issues about thinking. As you think through the organizing for success issues, pay attention to the actions needed to ensure that people are enhancing the thinking core competency by:

- Minimizing traditional blocks to thinking. (Chapter 1)
- Avoiding being stuck in paradigms. (Chapter 2)
- Maintaining an active spirit of inquiry. (Chapter 3)
- Designing meetings that promote collective thinking. (Chapter 4)
- Building an appropriate knowledge base. (Chapter 5)
- Using complementary modes of thought. (Chapter 6)
- Connecting complex and abstract thinking to focused and practical thinking. (Chapter 7)
- Sustaining a clear sense of the essential nature of any activity. (Chapter 8)
- Ensuring that thinking is always a complete process through the phases of perceiving, understanding, and reasoning. (Chapter 9)
- Flowing among a wide range of distinctive but related thought processes. (Chapter 10)

As you choose actions for the seven organizing issues, be sure that they support people working together successfully to implement strategic decisions, carry out marketing, operations, and research and development actions, and enhance the thinking core competency. Each issue that follows illustrates an important component of the manner in which strategy can enter the thinking about the way people work. Do not fall into the trap of simply describing things that sound nice or you would like to have in management of your organization. Management strategy is not about making things comfortable but about doing those things that best advance the strategy of your organization. Your management decisions must be consistent with the rest of your strategy.

1. Every organization has a culture with a foundation in core values. Cultures create predictability in the way people act and thereby can save time. You do not need to continually negotiate to establish ground rules for interaction among people. Cultures can also waste time as entrenched rules or procedures inhibit people's creativity and flexibility. The purpose of a culture is to serve the organization's strategic capability. An effective culture needs to enable the organization to rapidly respond to current and future market environment conditions. An effective culture feeds the ability of people to move into the future. Consider the actions necessary to create and sustain a culture consistent with your strategic ideas.

2. Your key strategic ideas will mandate some form of structure: a standard hierarchical style, matrix management, product-oriented organization, functionally oriented organization, or a process-centered organization. Choose a structure consistent with your strategy and identify the actions necessary to build that structure.

3. The key strategic ideas could lead to changes in culture or organization structure. Any new strategy or vision will represent a departure from the status quo. Therefore, actions to effectively manage change are necessary.

4. External relationships may be required to make your strategy successful. Therefore, consider actions to create and sustain the quality of relationship you want to have with suppliers, distributors, strategic partners, providers of complementary products, and competitors.

5. The key strategic ideas may require specific personnel strengths. Therefore, actions to hire, retain, and build those strengths are necessary. Frequently, there are key personnel, identifiable by name, who are critical to these strengths. In that context, consider actions you will take if these people leave the organization or if you have difficulty bringing critical high level skills into the organization.

6. Teams and collaborative work efforts are a current management hot topic. In a strategic sense, however, you want to address actions necessary to create the teams and other forms of internal collaboration critical to implementing the key strategic ideas.

7. Consider the actions necessary to build the core competencies critical to your strategy. Actions in this area include development and learning for existing personnel as well as actions to move new people into the flow of existing core competencies. Actions to enable you to evolve core competencies to meet the changing needs of the market and influence the evolution of that market are also relevant.

Pa$$ing the Buck Around

Finally, we arrive at the money. There will invariably be major corporate goals that are financial such as rates of return, profit levels, or revenue growth. The financial area is not so much an action area as a critical check on the way the whole strategy comes together. Too frequently people get caught in the numerical financial projections and lose some of the connections with the real business functions that these numbers measure. Traditional financial statements are less important than the following topics:

- Impact of strategy on revenues such as the effects of raising sales unit volumes, altering pricing structure, or entering new markets.
- Impact of strategy on cost structure—the ongoing resource commitments necessary to make the strategy work.

- Investments required to pursue strategy—the timing and sources of significant capital.
- Assumptions—the key reasons for believing the accuracy of physical sales levels, prices, physical resource commitments, and costs. All financial estimates begin with the resources—personnel, equipment, and materials—necessary for the product.
- Sensitivity analysis including break-even—to get a range of impacts from changes in the assumptions. There is an important chain of thinking that leads to the need for sensitivity analysis. A strategy represents the company's response to the most likely scenario for its future environment. That strategy leads to a wide range of actions with assumptions constantly being made. Therefore, it is necessary to vary these assumptions and determine when the feasibility of the strategy may be in question as well as when success could exceed expectations.
- Whole picture—what the dollars tell you about your strategy. This is the end of the strategic cycle and you may find from your financial analysis that you need to return to other parts of the cycle to change elements of your strategy.

EPILOGUE

Some Concluding Remarks

Many years ago, before I traveled across the country to attend Stanford's Graduate School of Business, my father, perhaps a little too gleefully, told me the following story:

> From their small business, a shoe store, this couple had managed to save enough money to give their son and daughter a college and postgraduate education. They both chose Harvard Business School. When they finished they returned home energized by all the wisdom they had learned and took over the store so their parents could retire. They used inventory control models, game theory, financial forecasting, and clever marketing techniques. They computerized the information systems, empowered the employees, organized teams, and instituted a performance-based salary system. They identified their core competencies and matched them to every conceivable scenario to prepare themselves for any future. Within 12 months they were bankrupt. They went to their parents saying, "We don't understand. We had the best business education. Yet, we failed at the business, while you managed to succeed for so many years. What's the problem?" The parents replied, "All we know is that we bought shoes for $10, sold them for $20 and made ourselves $10 per pair."

Regardless of the sophistication of our techniques or the cleverness of our jargon, some things remain unchanged. All we are trying to do is sell some product or service and make some profit along the way. Profit reflects the ability to make a difference in the eyes of the customers. It's that simple. The shoe store owners probably had the virtues of integrity, working hard, and focused minds set on using their business to help create their children's future. There's just one small catch. The quickening pace of technological change, the growing range and sophistication of consumer demands, and the globalization of business have caused us to realize tomorrow will not be like today. Profit motive and virtues, while necessary, are not sufficient. We try to restructure, downsize, merge, reengineer, form alliances, and transform. We turn every insightful idea into a mantra-filled fad, become cynical, lose interest, and jump on the next bandwagon.

Shared vision, shared values, empowerment, team-based work, just-in-time, quality, excellence, and world-class are among the numerous words that contain value but can become useless when they fade into jargon. You can always tell when an idea has descended to this level—people seem to use the words automatically, as a substitute for thinking or saying something more meaningful. There is a simple trick to move things out of jargon—ask what the words really mean. What do we mean when we say, *empowerment*? What does it mean to be *empowered*? How do we create that? We need to rekindle this willingness to ask questions—not to debate or make someone look foolish, but to fire up our brains to explore ideas, accept challenge, and put meaning back into our words.

Products come and go. Industries are born, grow, mature, and decline. It is similar to playing some ball game in which the rules keep shifting in the middle of play. We still have a ball, competitors, a field, and spectators but they seem to change all the time as well. One thing, however, will not change—keep your eye on the ball. In the game that matters, the ball is *thought*. Get outthought and the business cannot survive. If our thinking doesn't matter, then we don't matter.

Like all other business book writers, I want to sell you something. I don't have the secret for the best way to run your business, you do. I don't have an idea you can turn into a fad. I want to sell you the first of these abilities repeated throughout Hermann Hesse's book *Siddhartha*, "I can think. I can wait. I can fast." The other two can wait for future books. In business, the thinking that matters is the kind we ride into the future. Along with the profit motive and personal virtues of the shoe store story, thinking does not go out of style. It is not a fad that the next idea will replace; it is the fundamental capability that allows a sorting of ideas and the creation of new insights.

We have covered much terrain with a range of general thinking topics in the early part of the book and a variety of distinctive, but connected, processes for strategic thinking in the remainder of the book. I know you will find them useful, but none of the content requires memorization. It is all there to liberate thinking, especially from the knots of our own previous thoughts and experiences. We can choose only the future we are able to conceive. If we cannot think it, we cannot do it. We need thinking to expand way beyond the bounds of one perspective. The reality of our situation is a world of complexity, ambiguity, and uncertainty; we ignore it to our disadvantage. Flexible, wide-ranging, natural thinking is our best choice to turn reality to our advantage. The skeletal structure of strategic thinking is quite simple; it is the three questions from the Preface.

- What seems to be happening?
- What possibilities do we face?
- What are we going to do about it?

All we have done is add different kinds of ornaments to that structure. Each of the strategic thinking processes brings a different perspective and the possibility for different insights about one's business. Each of these processes also drives those insights toward some decision. We are thinking for the sake of acting deliberately and following the path we choose into the future. Each of the general thinking topics creates an orientation to extract the greatest potential from individual and collective intelligence. No business is going to thrive on the thoughts of one individual. Perhaps no business is worthwhile if it relegates people to tasks for which their thinking is irrelevant.

The Jar with the Dry Rim

The mind is an ocean . . . and so many worlds
are rolling there, mysterious, dimly seen!
And our bodies? Our body is a cup, floating
on the ocean; soon it will fill, and sink...
Not even one bubble will show where it went down.

The spirit is so near that you can't see it!
But reach for it . . . don't be a jar
full of water, whose rim is always dry.
Don't be the rider who gallops all night
and never sees the horse that is beneath him.

JELALUDDIN RUMI, *When Grapes Turn to Wine*
(Robert Bly, translator)

BIBLIOGRAPHY

Adams, Scott. *The Dilbert Principle: A Cubicle's Eye View of Bosses, Meetings, Management Fads and Other Workplace Afflictions.* New York: HarperCollins, 1996.

Albrecht, Karl. *The Northbound Train: Finding the Purpose, Setting the Direction, Shaping the Destiny of Your Organization.* New York: AMACOM, 1994.

Bly, Robert. *When Grapes Turn to Wine: Versions of Rumi.* Cambridge, Mass.: Yellow Moon Press, 1986.

Bohm, David. *On Dialogue,* edited by Lee Nichol. New York: Routledge, 1996.

————. *Unfolding Meaning: A Weekend of Dialogue with David Bohm.* New York: Routledge, 1996.

Hamel, Gary, and C. K. Prahalad. *Competing for the Future: Breakthrough Strategies for Seizing Control of Your Industry and Creating the Markets of Tomorrow.* Cambridge, Mass.: Harvard Business School Press, 1994.

Hammer, Michael. *Beyond Reengineering: How the Process-Oriented Organization Is Changing Our Work and Our Lives.* New York: HarperBusiness, 1996.

Hammer, Michael, and James Champy. *Reengineering the Corporation: A Manifesto for Business Revolution.* New York: HarperCollins, 1993.

Heidegger, Martin. *What Is Called Thinking?* New York: Harper and Row, 1968.

Hesse, Hermann. *Siddhartha.* New York: Bantam, 1971.

Hilmer, Frederick, and Lex Donaldson. *Management Redeemed: Debunking the Fads That Undermine Our Corporations.* New York: Free Press, 1996.

Jaworski, Joseph. *Synchronicity: The Inner Path of Leadership.* San Francisco: Berrett-Koehler Publishers, 1996.

Kahaner, Larry. *Competitive Intelligence: From Black Ops to Boardrooms—How Businesses Gather, Analyze and Use Information to Succeed in the Global Marketplace.* New York: Simon and Schuster, 1996.

Musahi, Miyamoto. *A Book of Five Rings: A Classic Guide to Strategy.* Woodstock, N.Y.: The Overlook Press, 1974.

Naisbitt, John, and Patricia Aburdene. *Megatrends 2000: Ten New Directions for the 1990s.* New York: Avon, 1996.

Nonaka, Ikujiro, and Hirotaka Takeuchi. *The Knowledge-Creating Company: How Japanese Companies Create the Dynamics of Innovation.* New York: Oxford University Press, 1995.

Pearson, Carol S., and Sharon Seivert. *Magic at Work: A Guide to Releasing Your Highest Creative Powers.* New York: Doubleday/Currency, 1995.

Popcorn, Faith, and Lys Marigold. *Clicking: 16 Trends to Future Fit Your Life, Your Work, and Your Business.* New York: HarperBusiness, 1996.

Rommel, Gunter, Jorgen Kluge, and Rolf-Dieter Kempis. *Simplicity Wins: How Germany's Mid-Sized Industrial Companies Succeed.* Cambridge, Mass.: Harvard Business School Press, 1995.

Schwartz, Peter. *The Art of the Long View: Planning for the Future in an Uncertain World.* New York: Doubleday/Currency, 1991.

Schumpeter, Joseph A. *Capitalism, Socialism, and Democracy.* New York: Harper Colophon, 1975.

Senge, Peter M. *The Fifth Discipline: The Art and Practice of the Learning Organization.* New York: Doubleday/Currency, 1990.

Simon, Hermann. *Hidden Champions: Lessons from 500 of the World's Best Unknown Companies.* Cambridge, Mass.: Harvard Business School Press, 1996.

Slywotzky, Adrian J. *Value Migration: How to Think Several Moves Ahead of the Competition.* Cambridge, Mass.: Harvard Business School Press, 1996.

Spitzer, Quinn, and Ron Evans. *Heads You Win: How the Best Companies Think.* New York: Simon and Schuster, 1997.

Stewart, Thomas A. *Intellectual Capital: The New Wealth of Organizations.* New York: Doubleday/Currency, 1997.

Sylvester, David. *Rene Magritte: Catalogue Raisonne.* London: Philip Wilson Publisher, 1992–1994.

Tzu, Lao. *Tao Te Ching.* New York: Penguin, 1963. (And the applications: John Heider, *The Tao of Leadership,* New York: Bantam, 1985; Bob Messing, *The Tao of Management,* Atlanta: Humanics New Age, 1989; Cresencio Torres, *The Tao of Teams,* San Diego, Calif.: Pfeiffer and Company, 1994.)

Tzu, Sun. *The Art of War.* New York: Oxford University Press, 1963.

Wells, Stuart. *From Sage to Artisan: The Nine Roles of the Value-Driven Leader.* Palo Alto, Calif.: Davies-Black Publishing, 1997.

Wheatley, Margaret J. *Leadership and the New Science: Learning about Organizations from an Orderly Universe.* San Francisco: Berrett-Koehler Publishers, 1992.

Whyte, David. *The Heart Aroused: Poetry and the Preservation of the Soul in Corporate America.* New York: Doubleday/Currency, 1994.

INDEX

Butterworth–Heinemann Business Books . . . for Transforming Business

5th Generation Management: Co-creating Through Virtual Enterprising, Dynamic Teaming, and Knowledge Networking, Revised Edition
Charles M. Savage, 0-7506-9701-6

After Atlantis: Working, Managing, and Leading in Turbulent Times
Ned Hamson, 0-7506-9884-5

The Alchemy of Fear: How to Break the Corporate Trance and Create Your Company's Successful Future
Kay Gilley, 0-7506-9909-4

Beyond Strategic Vision: Effective Corporate Action with Hoshin Planning
Michael Cowley and Ellen Domb, 0-7506-9843-8

Beyond Time Management: Business with Purpose
Robert A. Wright, 0-7506-9799-7

The Breakdown of Hierarchy: Communicating in the Evolving Workplace
Eugene Marlow and Patricia O'Connor Wilson, 0-7056-9746-6

Business and the Feminine Principle: The Untapped Resource
Carol R. Frenier, 0-7506-9829-2

Choosing the Future: The Power of Strategic Thinking
Stuart Wells, 0-7506-9876-4

Cultivating Common Ground: Releasing the Power of Relationships at Work
Daniel S. Hanson, 0-7506-9832-2

Flight of the Phoenix: Soaring to Success in the 21st Century
John Whiteside and Sandra Egli, 0-7506-9798-9

Getting a Grip on Tomorrow: Your Guide to Survival and Success in the Changed World of Work
Mike Johnson, 0-7506-9758-X

Innovation Strategy for the Knowledge Economy: The Ken Awakening
Debra M. Amidon, 0-7506-9841-1

The Intelligence Advantage: Organizing for Complexity
Michael D. McMaster, 0-7506-9792-X

Intuitive Imagery: A Resource at Work
John B. Pehrson and Susan E. Mehrtens, 0-7506-9805-5

The Knowledge Evolution: Expanding Organizational Intelligence
Verna Allee, 0-7506-9842-X

Leadership in a Challenging World: A Sacred Journey
Barbara Shipka, 0-7506-9750-4

Leading Consciously: A Pilgrimage Toward Self-Mastery
Debashis Chatterjee, 0-7506-9864-0

Leading from the Heart: Choosing Courage over Fear in the Workplace
Kay Gilley, 0-7506-9835-7

Learning to Read the Signs: Reclaiming Pragmatism in Business
F. Byron Nahser, 0-7506-9901-9

Leveraging People and Profit: The Hard Work of Soft Management,
Bernard A. Nagle and Perry Pascarella, 0-7506-9961-2

Marketing Plans That Work: Targeting Growth and Profitability
Malcolm H. B. McDonald and Warren J. Keegan, 0-7506-9828-4

A Place to Shine: Emerging from the Shadows at Work
Daniel S. Hanson, 0-7506-9738-5

Power Partnering: A Strategy for Business Excellence in the 21st Century
Sean Gadman, 0-7506-9809-8

Putting Emotional Intelligence to Work: Successful Leadership Is More Than IQ
David Ryback, 0-7506-9956-6

Resources for the Knowledge-Based Economy Series
> *The Knowledge Economy*
> Dale Neef, 0-7506-9936-1

> *Knowledge Management and Organizational Design*
> Paul S. Myers, 0-7506-9749-0

> *Knowledge Management Tool*
> Rudy L. Ruggles, III, 0-7506-9849-7

> *Knowledge in Organization*
> Laurence Prusak, 0-7506-9718-0

> *The Strategic Management of Intellectual Capital*
> David A. Klein, 0-7506-9850-0

The Rhythm of Business: The Key to Building and Running Successful Companies
Jeffrey C. Shulman, 0-7506-9991-4

Setting the PACE® in Product Development: A Guide to Product and Cycle-time Excellence
Michael E. McGrath, 0-7506-9789-X

Time to Take Control: The Impact of Change on Corporate Computer Systems
Tony Johnson, 0-7506-9863-2

The Transformation of Management
Mike Davidson, 0-7506-9814-4

What Is the Emperor Wearing? Truth-Telling in Business Relationships
Laurie Weiss, 0-7506-9872-1

Who We Could Be at Work, Revised Edition
Margaret A. Lulic, 0-7506-9739-3

Working from Your Core: Personal and Corporate Wisdom in a World of Change
Sharon Seivert, 0-7506-9931-0

To purchase any Butterworth–Heinemann title, please visit your local bookstore or call 1-800-366-2665.

Stuart Wells is Professor of Organization and Management at San Jose State University, where he has served as Director of the Center for Global Competitiveness and Director of the Small Business Institute. As founder of the Leading Edge Consulting Group and cofounder of Corporate Wisdom, he has worked on leadership development and strategy issues with such major corporations as Clorox, Crown-Zellerbach, Dupont, Pacific Telesis, PepsiCo, and Proctor and Gamble. He is the author of *From Sage to Artisan: The Nine Roles of the Value-Driven Leader* and developed several assessment instruments to analyze individual and team preferences for the nine roles described in the book.

He has also consulted with numerous international agencies— UNESCO, U.S. Agency for International Development, Stanford Research Institute, National Institute for Education, and the Federal Council for Science and Technology as well as several governments throughout Africa, Asia, and Latin America. In conjunction with this work he has authored 6 books and more than 20 articles.

He has a Mechanical Engineering degree from the City University of New York and an MBA, MA in Economics, and Ph.D. from the Stanford Graduate School of Business and Department of Economics.

If you would like to contact Dr. Wells, please write to him at:

Leading Edge Consulting Group
P.O. Box 67
Saratoga, CA 95071-0067

e-mail: ldngedge@pacbell.net